THE UNIVERSITY OF OXFORD

A Brief History

DOMI: NUS ILLU:
MINA: TIO MEA
DOMI: NUS ILLU:
MINA: TIO MEA
DOMI: NUS ILLU:
MINA: TIO MEA

THE UNIVERSITY OF OXFORD
A Brief History

Laurence Brockliss

Bodleian Library
UNIVERSITY OF OXFORD

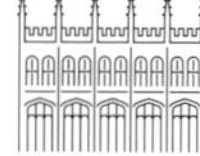

First published in 2019 by Bodleian Library Publishing
Broad Street, Oxford OX1 3BG
www.bodleianshop.co.uk

2nd impression 2023

ISBN: 978 1 85124 500 0

Image opposite title page: The University's coat of arms – 'God is my enlightenment' – in use from the late thirteenth century and depicted here on the ceiling of Duke Humfrey's Library.

Cover design by Dot Little at the Bodleian Library
Designed and typeset by Laura Parker in 9.8 on 15.2 Foundry Wilson
Printed and bound in China by 1010 Printing International Ltd. on 157gsm Matt Art paper

British Library Catalogue in Publishing Data
A CIP record of this publication is available from the British Library

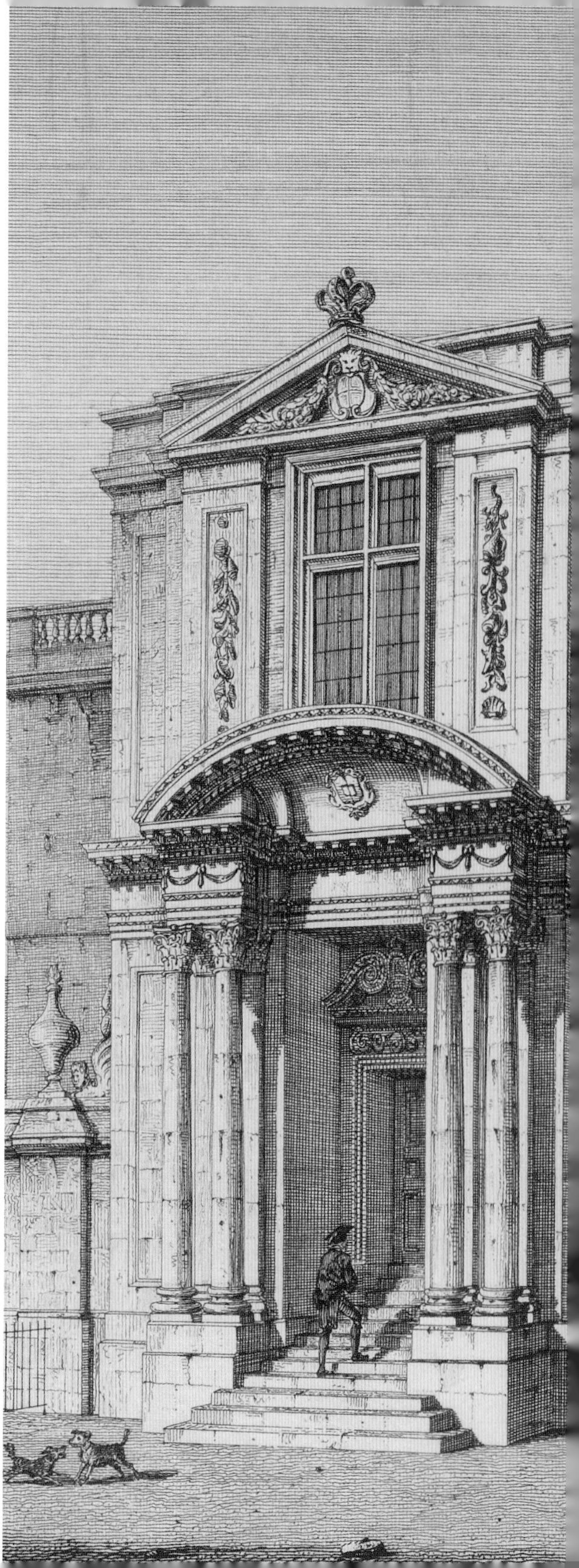

CONTENTS

Foreword

Oxford is the third oldest university in Europe. Although it was not founded by Alfred the Great as was frequently asserted before the nineteenth century, it has certainly existed since the reign of King John. It is as old as Magna Carta, older than Parliament and far older than the Church of England. Cambridge, with which it is usually coupled, is its junior by only a few years, but it was its offspring, not an independent foundation. When a visitor to the city stands on the High Street and watches the chancellor, vice-chancellor, college heads and senior members of the university process in their caps and gowns to St Mary the Virgin, the university's church, or to the Sheldonian Theatre for Encaenia,[1] it must be tempting to think that Oxford is little changed from the Middle Ages. In fact, the university has never stood still; it has always evolved; and today's Oxford has little in common with the university of the first half of the twentieth century, let alone earlier eras.

This short introduction to an institution nearly as old as the monarchy takes the reader on a swift journey through Oxford's 800-year history from its beginnings until the present day. It is divided into four chapters, each chapter describing a distinct period in the university's life. The first deals with the medieval university when Oxford, at least until 1400, was one of the leading centres of learning of western Christendom. The second looks at the changes wrought by the Reformation,

Joseph Mallord William Turner, *View of the High Street, Oxford*, 1809–10.

which turned Oxford (and Cambridge) into an arm of the English monarchy and the new Church of England, brought the colleges to the fore, and led to a period of 300 years in which most of the university descended into an intellectual slumber. The third chapter explores the period between the 1850s and the outbreak of the Second World War, when Oxford was prodded into new life by parliamentary fiat; opened its doors to non-Anglicans, women and subjects of the British Empire; laid the foundations of the modern tutorial system; and began belatedly to take an interest in the advancement and not just the dissemination of knowledge. The final chapter explores the emergence of the modern world-class research university which developed after 1945. Much larger, richer and vibrant than in any other period of its history, this is the Oxford of today which lies behind the facade of the old buildings that tourists come to see. A visitor who wants to grasp the present reality should take a walk round the Science Area, not the complex of architectural masterpieces that lie between St Mary's on the High and the Clarendon Building on the Broad.

A short introduction can only touch the surface. It is hoped that it will tempt the reader to turn to some of the more detailed works listed in Further Reading. It will have served its purpose if it helps visitors to understand that Oxford is certainly not and never was the university of Morse and Lewis, but somewhere much more interesting and important in the history of our nation and the history of the world.

Encaenia procession, 2015: the day each year when the university remembers its benefactors.

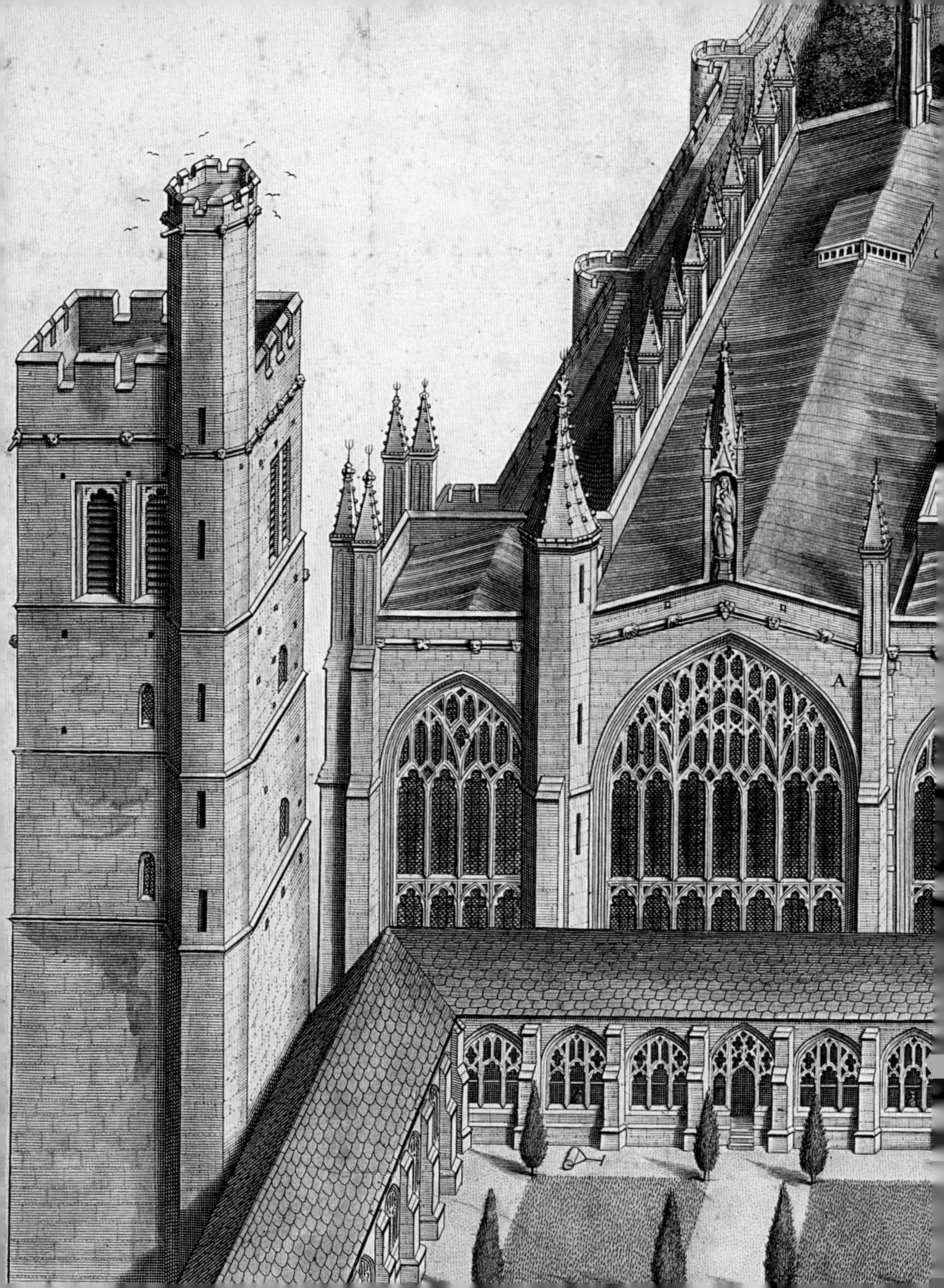
A

The Medieval University

BEGINNINGS

Higher studies have been taught at Oxford in some form since *c.*1095, when an itinerant Frenchman called Theobald of Étampes set up a school of philosophy in the town, which he maintained for at least twenty years. Little is known about the history of higher learning in Oxford over the following century, but it is clear that Theobald's initiative inspired others to follow his example. By the turn of the thirteenth century, individual teachers or masters were giving courses in theology and law as well as philosophy, among them the future Archbishop of Canterbury and saint, Edmund of Abingdon (*c.*1170–1240). At this stage, Oxford's schools had no collective identity. They were no different from similar schools of higher learning that had been founded since the middle of the eleventh century all over western Europe, as the Roman Church, after six centuries of indifference, once again began to value the spirit of enquiry. In fact, they were not even the most famous in England. The most successful of the new schools were attached to rich cathedrals or abbeys or established in bustling centres of commerce and administration. Oxford's had none of these advantages. In 1200 it was a small market and county town on the north bank of the Thames with perhaps 4,000 inhabitants. It had a town council, a castle and a royal palace, but it was only the seat of an archdeacon, not of a bishop. The chief thing that attracted masters to establish a school in the town was the archdeacon's court. As this dealt with juicy disputes involving local abbeys and cases appealed to Rome that the papal curia referred back, there was a ready student audience to be found among the floating population of clergy and ecclesiastical lawyers continually drawn to the town.

Oxford's schools began to be differentiated from their rivals only in 1214. Five years earlier, two students suspected of murder were hanged on the order of the town's magistrate. In

Bull of Nicholas de Romanis, papal legate, 20 June 1214: the earliest document to recognize the university as an institution with a collective identity.

Nichol dei gra Tuscul eps Aplice Sedis Legatus. Omnib xpi fidelib sal in dno. Universitati vre notum facim qd cu
burgenses Oxon p suspendio clericor qd comiserant mandatis ecclie p omia satisfacere iurassent: nos volentes agere misericordit cum eisdem:
statuim qd a festo Sci Michael anno ab Incarnatione dni Millesimo ducentesimo quartodecimo usq in decem annos sequentes sco
laribus Oxon studentib condonet medietas mercedis hospitior omnium locandor clericis in eadem villa. mercedis inquam taxate communi
consilio clericor et burgensium an recessum scolarium ppt pdcm suspendium clericor. Finitis vo pdcis decem annis: aliis decem annis
proxo sequentib locabunt hospitia sic mercede olim ut pdcm est taxata. Hec de hospitiis constructis et taxatis an pfatum recessum clericor.
Constructa vo postmodum vel construenda aliaq pst constructa s n taxata: arbitrio quatuor magistror et quatuor burgensium taxabunt et p
dicto in p terminu decennium locabunt. Communa qq eiusdem ville annuatim in ppetuum dabit quinquaginta duos solid dispensandos in
usus pauperum scolarium p manu Abbis de Oseny et prioris Sce Frithesswith de consilio venabilis fris Hug tunc Linc epi et successor
suor vel archidi loci seu officialis ei aut cancellarii quem eps Linc ibidem scolaribus pficiet. Ita scilicet qd viginti sex sol solvent
annuatim i festo omnium Scor. et viginti sex sol. in capite ieiunii. et hoc faciet communa p se vel p alium: vice ei illud facientem. pa
bit etiam eadem communa vel alii vice ipius pascet centu paupes scolares in pane. et cervisia. potagio. et uno ferculo piscium vel carnium.
singulis annis in ppetuum die Sci Nichol. qm eps Linc vel archids loci seu officialis ei aut ipe cancellarius vel alii ad hoc ab epo
Linc deputati, puidint. Iurabunt etiam pfati burgenses qd victualia iusto et rationabili pcio scolaribus vendent. et ad ut alia necessaria
eis clarius qm aliis. vendi no pmittabunt. et qd in fraudem h provisionis fraus no facient constitutiones vel onosas. p qs clericor conditio
deterioret. Si vo contingat aliquem clericu a laicis capi: statim cu fuint sup eo requisiti ab epo Linc vel archido loci seu ei officiali vel a can
cellario seu ab eo quem eps Linc huic offo deputaverit: captum ei reddent scdm debitum regni et ecclie consuetudinem. n aliq in machina
buntur in hiis vel aliis: p qd epi iurisdictio eludat. vel ius suum vel ecclie sue i aliq minuat. Iurabunt aut quinquaginta de maioribus Oxon
p se et communa et quantu in eis est. p heredibus suis qd hec omnia suprdca fidelit observabunt. et hoc iuramentu qlibet anno renovabunt ad
mandatum epi Linc p qt idem eps voluit eis nuntium pmittere. Cartam quoq sigillo commune signatam sup pdcis articulis facient pdci
burgenses et epo Linc tradabunt cui voluit in custodia committendam. Hac aut facient pdci burgenses et heredes eor. in clericis honor et re
verentia eo exhibeat habundanti: q magis p eos pfundit dehonestati. Magri vo q post recessu scolarium irreverent legunt Oxon suspen
dent p triennium ab offo legendi ibidem. Omes aut q de suspendio clericor confessi fuerunt vel convicti: venient humilit ad mandatu epi
Linc cu interdictum fuit relaxatum: ad sepulcra clericor discalciati et disincti sine capis et palliis sequente eos communa. et ipoz corpa deferent
cu honore et reverentia i cimiterio sepelienda. ubi clerus puidit. Postea q ut pdcm est a memoratis burgensib iuramto et carta commune
confecta et epo Linc tradita. licentiam habebunt scolares et magri Oxon redeundi et ibide legendi: exceptis hiis q p triennium sunt suspensi:
de qbus est pmissum. Si vo pdci burgenses contra statuta nra et ppium venint iuramtu. ex tpo facto se sciant excomicationis vinculo innodatos.
et eps Linc vel successores sui eos et villam eor reducant i pristinam suspensionis sntiam. Dat apd Sempringeham. xii. kl Iul.

Robert Grosseteste, bishop of Lincoln (d.1253): philosopher, theologian and the university's first prominent chancellor, 1224–31.

retaliation the teachers and their students abandoned Oxford and went elsewhere, including to Cambridge where schools of higher learning were founded for the first time. The student population by then must have been an important source of wealth for the town because the burgesses eventually sued for peace and begged the papal legate then in the country, Nicholas de Romanis, cardinal bishop of Tusculum (d.1218), to arrange terms. The legate's subsequent bull settling the dispute, promulgated on 20 June 1214, gave the returning masters and students of Oxford a collective and independent identity for the first time. Henceforth, they were to be given immunity from lay jurisdiction, and their representatives were to have a say in fixing the cost of rents and food. Above all, the bull made provision for the appointment by the local diocesan, the bishop of Lincoln, of an official who would look after their rights, called the scholars' chancellor.[2] Thereafter the masters and students had a rudimentary organization and an embryonic legal personality. The Oxford schools had taken the first steps to becoming a *universitas*, a Latin word for a corporation that gradually came to be used only in connection with institutions of higher learning. Only two of Europe's existing schools had hitherto attained this dignity – those of Bologna and Paris – and both were in significant cities, not a provincial backwater.

GROWTH

In the next century and a half, Oxford's schools capitalized on this stroke of good fortune and greatly enhanced their independence. The key figure in the university's early years was the master Robert Grosseteste (*c.*1175/9–1253). From 1224 until his death, first as the university's chancellor, then as a teacher of theology, and finally as bishop of Lincoln, he worked energetically to ensure the new institution was placed on a solid footing. Thanks to the support of both the church and the crown, Grosseteste and his successors, as the scholars' chancellor, were able slowly to extend the jurisdiction of the office so that from 1290 virtually all disputes between townsmen and scholars, both civil and criminal, were brought within its ambit. As town–gown riots were frequent, each altercation led to a strengthening of the university's position.

After a pitched battle on St Scholastica's day 1355, King Edward III issued a royal charter which all but handed the town over to the chancellor: he was charged with assaying the weights and measures used in commercial transactions, maintaining the town's buildings in good repair and even cleaning the streets. In England only the newly founded schools at Cambridge gained similar privileges, so the others extant in 1200, unsurprisingly, withered away and Oxford reigned supreme. No matriculation register exists for the medieval university but around 1300 there may have been as many as 2,000 masters and students in Oxford, all of them men, who probably formed more than half the adult population in what was still a small town.[3]

By the mid fourteenth century the University of Oxford was a fully fledged corporation with its own seal and coat of arms. The chancellor, who was a resident master, was the undisputed head of the corporation and usually served for two years. Although initially an appointee of the bishop of Lincoln, he soon become an elected official, and from 1367 could take up office without episcopal approval. He was assisted in running the university by a number of other officials. Most important were the two annually elected proctors who, from at least 1267–8, oversaw teaching, kept law and order, and organized the institution's ceremonial life. The election of officials and decisions concerning the university were taken by the masters meeting collectively in a body. The *congregatio magna* contained all the resident masters, the *congregatio minor* only the regents or those actually teaching. When it was felt necessary, the masters' decisions were turned into statutes or university law.[4] For many years the university had no building of its own in which to meet. From the 1320s, however, through the generosity of Thomas Cobham (d.1327), bishop of Worcester, it had its own congregation house. This was a two-storey building attached to the north wall of the chancel of the church of St Mary

Merton College, Mob Quad, mid fourteenth century: Oxford's first purpose-built quadrangle, erected in its oldest college, founded in 1274.

OVERLEAF
University College, officially inaugurated in 1280: Oxford's second oldest college. Print from David Loggan, *Oxonia Illustrata* (1675).

the Virgin on the High Street, whose upper floor housed the university's small library of manuscript books.

The university in 1350 offered teaching in five subjects or faculties: arts (rhetoric and philosophy), theology, canon law, civil law and medicine. The curriculum was built around a series of texts: the Aristotelian corpus; the Bible and the *Sentences* of Peter Lombard; Gratian's *Decretum* and the papal *Decretals*; the *Code* and the *Digest*; and an assortment of Greek, Arab and Jewish medical authors.[5] Students in each case followed the prescribed curriculum for a specified time, after which they were eligible to demonstrate the fruits of their learning before their teachers and show they had the ability to teach in their own right. The examination was in three

COLLEGI
A. Capella
B. Bibliotheca
C. Refectorium
D. Magistri Hospitiū
D. Loggan delin. et Sculp. cum Privil S.R.M.
Circa An: Sal: 872 Alfredus sive Alvredus Occidentalium Saxonum Rex vere magnus pene intermortua literar
pergeret) hospitem, e Gallia accersivit. Qui consilio et sumptu Regis Collegiū hoc (hodie Magnæ Aulæ Universitatis appellati
reditibus tam pro Professoribus quam studiosis, dotavit Quibus postea, Danorū Normannorumq; invasione bellisq; civili
ratum, & aliorum (maxima ex parte Alumnorū suorum) Gualteri scilicet Skirlaw Episcopi Dunelmensis, Henrici Northu
statum evectū fuit. In quo Magister, Socij 12, Exhibitionarij (munere honoratissimi Roberti Comitis Leicestriæ dotali) 2; una cū
Magistrū constitutum, primumq; Sociū Stum Ioannē de Bevertaco, tulit hoc Collegiū S. Edmundum, Richardū Armachanum, Georgiū Abbo

RSITATIS
Illustrissimo D.no
FRANCISCO BRUDENELL
Honoratissimi Roberti
Comitis de Cardigan
filio natu maximo
vetustissimi hujus
Collegij tabellam
hanc D.D.C.Q
Dav. Loggan
E F. pedes 150.
C
F

resuscitaturus Grimoaldū sive Grimbaldum, virum sanctitate et doctrina celebrem nec non Regis (dum Romam
ıæ alia Philosophiæ et Grammaticæ destinata, fundavit; et liberalibus stipendijs; primū e fisco regio dein e certis fundorum
giū desolationē, & tantum non ruinā, passum est. Donec Gulielmi Archidiaconi Dunelmensis pietate refectū, & instau-
Perciorū stirpe, Comitis Secundi, Caroli Greenwood, et D.ni Simonis Benet, aliorumq liberalitate auctum, et in præsentem
ıribus, servientibus, & ministris, in honorē Dei et augmentū Cleri honeste sustentantur. Præter S. Grimbaldu ab Alfrēdo
hiepiscopos; Richardū Fleming Episcopū Lincolniensem; aliosq plurimos, tum vitæ sanctitate tum scriptis celeberrimos.

Roger Bacon (c.1214–1294): Franciscan polymath and experimentalist, Oxford's most original medieval philosopher.

steps or stages (hence the term 'degree'). A student first became a bachelor (or aspirant), then a licentiate (someone who had proved his worth) and finally a doctor or master (a qualified expert in his subject), who was then expected to spend a number of years as a teacher. A bachelor's degree was awarded simply on evidence of fulfilling a required period of study. The licence and doctorate, however, were bestowed only after the candidate had shown his ability to lecture and shown intellectual agility in a number of disputations or public debates. Obtaining a doctor's degree in any faculty was a lengthy and complicated process. As students were normally expected to graduate as a master of arts before they moved on to study in another or higher faculty, by the time a doctor of theology had served as a regent the scholar would have spent nearly twenty years in the university.

All the students and masters were priests or in minor orders, for the university was an arm of the church, even if some of its graduates ended up in the royal administration. Initially, they found digs in citizens' houses and were known as 'chamberdeacons'.[6] But by the mid fourteenth century a growing number were living in student hostels or halls. These were buildings rented out by the year to masters and run for profit. The name reflected the fact that the inhabitants took their meals together in a common dining room. A minority of scholars by then also had their board and lodgings paid for. Some, who were friars, lived in the convents of the mendicant orders which had already been established in Oxford for over a century. Others, who belonged to the contemplative orders, were housed in the various abbeys and monasteries in and around the town. The rest lived in a new institution, the college, which was an endowed hall, established by charter and owning its site. By 1350 there were eight in existence. Two, Durham and Gloucester colleges, were set up for Benedictine students in 1289 and 1298, respectively. The others were established by wealthy churchmen, often close to the crown, to support the studies of poor secular clerics. The first to be founded was Merton in 1274, followed by University College (1280), Balliol (1282), Exeter (*c.*1314), Oriel (1324) and Queen's (1341). Each secular college through its endowment maintained a number of scholars and chaplains from a particular part of the country, who not only took meals together but lived under a common semi-monastic discipline and several times a day joined each other in prayer. The colleges were self-governing corporations whose management was in the hands of the students supported on the foundation. Known as *socii*, or in English 'fellows', these were usually graduates in arts engaged in higher studies, and each fellow played a part in the election of new members of the foundation and the college head.[7]

Oxford in the mid fourteenth century was only one of about thirty-five universities in Europe, but despite its provincial

Distat ab Oxonio spatijs Exonia multis,
Et procul occiduu vergit ad ora maris.
Attamen Oxonij sedes Exonia fixas
Invenit, et musis iam fit amica quies.
Condidit has Præsul Gualterus Stapleton ædes.
Indidit et sedi nomina digna suæ.

Exeter College, founded c.1314: established for students from the south-west of England. From John Bereblock, *Luna: An Illustrated Guide to Oxford University* (1566).

setting it was among the most prestigious because of the fertility and originality of its teaching in philosophy and theology. In the thirteenth century, Paris had been the home of the most creative thinkers, above all Thomas Aquinas (1224/5–1274), who had shown how the truths of reason embodied in Aristotle might be reconciled with the truths of faith upheld by the church. The only Oxford scholar with an international reputation was the Franciscan friar Roger Bacon (*c.*1214–1294), who believed that humans could ultimately control the natural world if they developed a new science of nature based on observation and experiment. At the turn of the fourteenth century, however, the torch passed to Oxford. In John Duns Scotus (*c.*1265–*c.*1308) and William of Ockham (d.*c.*1349), two other Franciscans, the university produced a pair of intellectual giants. Duns Scotus appreciated the efforts of Aquinas but argued that he made too much of human reason: God was beyond our human understanding. Ockham went even further and claimed that we could know nothing at all for certain: abstract entities were human constructions and all judgements were contingent. Together with Aquinas, they created the three *viae*, or pathways, which dominated philosophical teaching in Europe for the rest of the Middle Ages. The university in the first half of the fourteenth century also sheltered a clutch of highly creative linguistic philosophers called terminists, who explored the complex role and meaning of words in particular contexts. As many of them were fellows of Merton College they became known as the Mertonians. Some of the group, notably Thomas Bradwardine (*c.*1290–1349), became especially interested in propositions about motion and change and began to consider how speed and velocity might be expressed quantitatively.

Oxford's nascent organization mirrored the system of governance in most of the universities north of the Alps.

These were all masters' universities where the students had no control. What was singular about both Oxford and Cambridge was that the subject faculties never evolved into separate corporations: they remained clusters of doctors and masters. Nor did the two English universities possess nations or legally recognized regional associations of students or masters gathered together for their own protection. Oxford and Cambridge also enjoyed peculiarly extensive privileges. Nowhere else did the chancellor or his equivalent have such wide powers over both the scholars and the local town.

MATURITY

The university's structure altered little between 1350 and the Reformation. By the early sixteenth century the chancellor had become a permanent official and the office was held by a bishop based at the king's court. As a result, his day-to-day duties came to be performed by a deputy or vice-chancellor. The roles of the two assemblies of masters were also slowly clarified. The *congregatio magna* eventually assumed the mantle of the university's legislature and became the place where major decisions were taken. About 1500 it began to be called 'Convocation'. The *congregatio minor* was thereafter left with day-to-day administrative matters as its remit and took the title 'Congregation'. Otherwise nothing changed. On the Continent, by the end of the fifteenth century lay students were flocking into the faculties of civil law to gain the training they needed to serve in the expanding system of secular courts. But Oxford remained a university of clerics. In England the king's courts used common not Roman law and secular lawyers learnt their trade in the London Inns.

Nevertheless the university continued to evolve in the Late Middle Ages. In the first place, town and gown were on much

Congregation House, built in the 1320s as a place where the university's masters could discuss academic business. Print from Anthony Wood, *The History and Antiquities of the Colleges and Halls in the University of Oxford*, ed. J. Gutch (1786–90).

better terms than before and there were no longer any major fracas. This was partly because there were fewer students. After 1400 Cambridge, hitherto in its elder sister's shadow, began to expand and numbers at Oxford fell, perhaps by as much as a third. Mainly, peace between the two sides was achieved by largely keeping them apart. The university became convinced that the cause of the periodic and bloody unrest lay with the chamberdeacons, who were judged to be lazy, lewd and ill-disciplined. It was decided to solve the problem by excising the 'putrid limb'. From about 1410 all students and masters were ordered to live in a hall or college where they could experience the benefits of communal living.[8] The masters of the halls, just like the college heads, were expected to ensure that their tenants lived in a manner befitting their clerical status. In the course of the 1480s all of the halls were made subject to a common disciplinary statute. Tenants had to attend daily mass, dress and speak decently, and not 'indulge in games of chance or dice, hand-ball, sword play or any other dishonest game'. They could go out into the town but only at times permitted by the master of the hall.[9]

More importantly for the future history of the university, by the 1530s the colleges had moved from the periphery to its heart. In the interim, seven more secular colleges had been established by prominent churchmen: New College (1379), Lincoln (1427), All Souls (1438), Magdalen (1458), Brasenose (1509), Corpus Christi (1517) and Cardinal (1525), the foundation of Henry VIII's right-hand man, Thomas Wolsey (*c.*1475–1530). Two further regular colleges were also created: Frewen Hall (for Augustinian canons) and St Bernard's (for Cistercians). As a result, there were far more students receiving free board and lodging than hitherto, especially as New College, Magdalen and Cardinal were conceived as huge foundations. There were also many more young students within their walls, for most of the new foundations made provision for the support of a significant number of arts students who were not yet bachelors and were known as scholars to distinguish them from the older fellows.[10] Nonetheless, towards the end of the fifteenth century the secular colleges still housed only a minority of students. The position changed very quickly in the next thirty years as the colleges began to admit paying boarders. The first to do so was Magdalen, which was specifically

Wycliffite Bible, the first translation of the Bible into English by the radical Oxford theologian John Wyclif (d.1384) and his university supporters. The page shows the beginning of the Romans, late fourteenth and early fifteenth century.

self to þee. whanne þou
e. þou girdidist þee & wa-
e þou woldist/ but
u schalt waxe elder. þ
de forþ þin hondis: &
l girde þee & schal lede
r þou wolt not/ he sei-
gnyfiynge bi what deeþ
glorifie god. And whanne
seid þese þingis: he seiþ
ou me/ petir turnede and
sciple suynge. whom ihc
ich also restide in þe so-
brest: & he seide to him/
s it þat schal bitraie þee/
e petir hadde seen þis:
hu/ lord but what þis:
m/ so I wole þat he dwel-
come/ what to þee: sue
for þis word wente out
en: þat þilke dis-
ot/ & ihc seide not to him/ þat
: but so I wole þat he
come. what to þee/ þis
sciple. þat beriþ witnes-
þingis & wroot hem & we

to fore þe pistil to romayns

Romayns ben in þe cuntre
of ytalie. þei weren disse-
ued first of false prophetis;
þat is fals techers/ & vndir þe name
of oure lord ihu crist: þei weren brouȝt
in to þe lawe & prophetis. þat is in to
ceremonyes eþer fleischli kepinge of
moises lawe. & of prophetis. acor-
dinge wiþ þo cerymonyes: which v-
singe is now contrarie. to þe truþe
& fredom of cristis gospel/ Poul a-
ȝenclepiþ þese romayns to verri feiþ
& truþe of þe gospel: & writiþ to
hem þis pistil fro corinthe. Ierom
seiþ þis in his prolog to romayns
Here bigynneþ þe firste chapitre.

Poul þe ser-
uaunt of
ihu crist:
clepid an
apostil/ se-
parid in
to þe gos-
pel of god:
which he hadde bihote to fore bi his

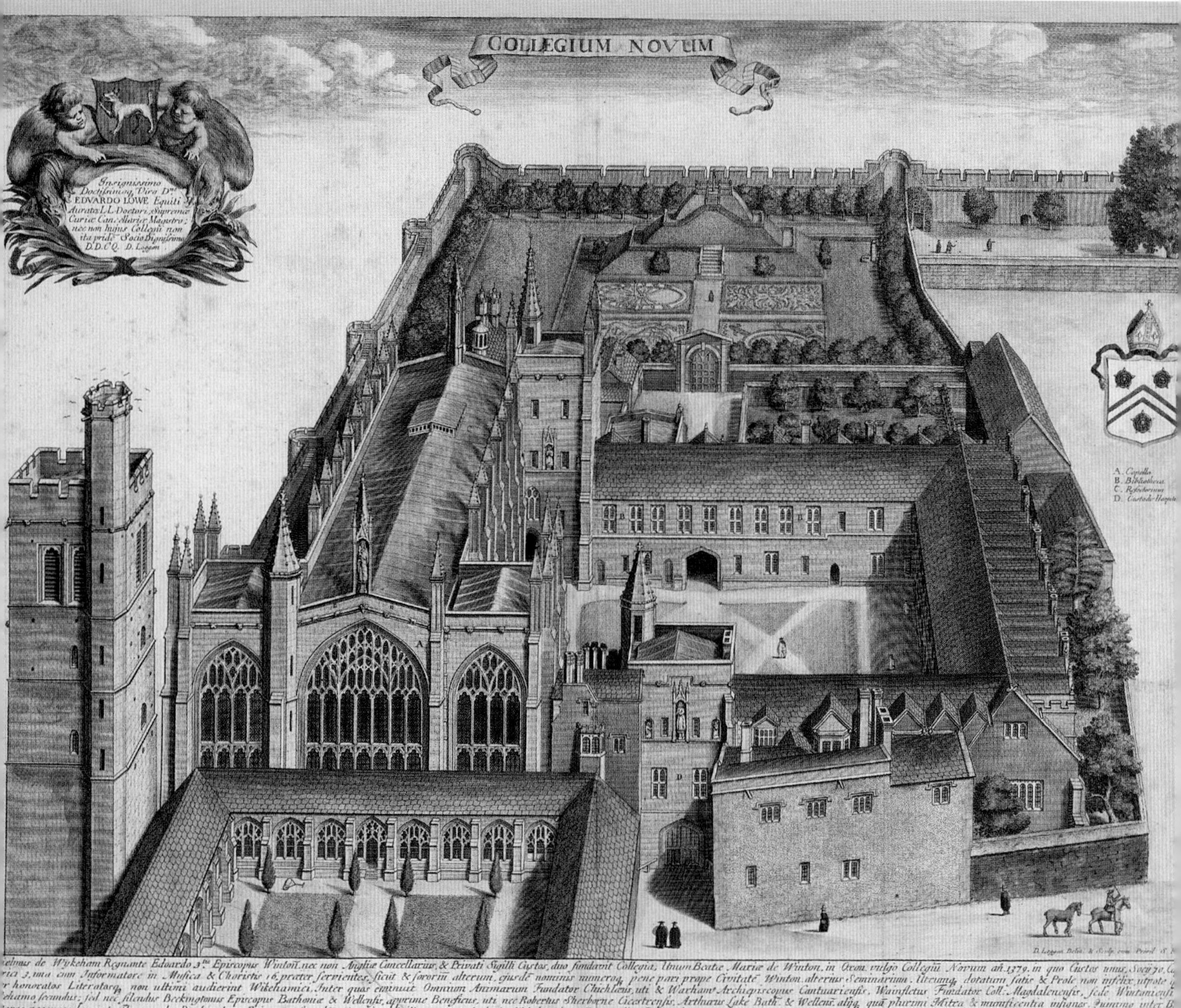
COLLEGIUM NOVUM
Insignissimo Doctissimoq; Viro Dno EDVARDO LOWE Equiti Aurato L.L. Doctori Supremae Curiae Cancellariae Magistro; nec non hujus Collegii non ita pridem Socio Dignissimo D.D.C.Q. D. Loggan
A. Capella
B. Bibliotheca
C. Refectorium
D. Custodis Hospit

New College: Oxford's first large college, founded in 1379 for students from Winchester School. Print from David Loggan, *Oxonia Illustrata* (1675).

permitted under its 1480 statutes to accept up to twenty offspring of 'noblemen and worthy commoners'.[11] By the 1530s most of the other colleges appear to have followed suit, and twenty years later the revolution was complete. In 1552 a head count by the vice-chancellor revealed that three-quarters of the student body were living within a college.[12] The transformation had a dramatic effect on the number of halls. There were sixty-six halls in the 1540s and only eight a century later.

The colleges' new status was matched by their growing physical presence in the urban landscape. The university had little money and its regent masters for the most part taught, as they had always done, in rented rooms. By the 1530s it had erected only one further building: a theology or divinity school. The decision was taken to erect the school in 1423 but it took fifty years to raise the funds. The two-storey building constructed by the Oxford master mason William Orchard (d.1504), with its fine van vaulting and upper library to house the books given to the university by Humfrey, duke of Gloucester (1391–1447), was not completed until 1488. The colleges, however, were richer and showed more ambition. The first foundations were mostly set up in buildings that their benefactors had purchased in the town. But Merton, from the beginning, made alterations to its site. As early as the 1280s it started work on its huge chapel and in the mid fourteenth century constructed Oxford's first purpose-built college quadrangle, Mob Quad. Merton thereafter set the tone. By the 1530s all the colleges had made some attempt to build anew, and a number of the later foundations were handsomely housed by benefactors anxious to leave their mark. New College had a purpose-built quadrangle, chapel, dining hall and library from 1403, All Souls from 1442 and Magdalen from 1480. In the fifteenth century every college tried to outshine the others. Those that could afford it put up grandiose Gothic

Magdalen College tower, c.1500: a slightly later addition to a college founded initially in 1458 and set up on a new site with a large endowment in 1480. Print from William Combe, *A History of the University of Oxford* (published by Ackermann, 1814).

gateways and towers, constructed in the new late Perpendicular style. Magdalen went one stage further and at the turn of the sixteenth century erected a 144-foot bell tower that had no obvious function except to advertise the college's wealth and prestige. Unsurprisingly, then, given the opportunity, students preferred to live in a college than in a hall: most colleges in the early sixteenth century offered better-quality accommodation.

Neither development, however, burnished the university's intellectual credentials, as after 1400 Oxford ceased to be a philosophical and theological powerhouse. The most able minds in the university felt that their primary task was to educate good priests and preachers, not skilful debaters, and that the exploration of the thorny problems that had fired the interest of Duns Scotus and his successors served no purpose. By the turn of the sixteenth century, too, some masters had come under the influence of the Renaissance Italian humanists, who wanted students to be taught to write and speak good classical Latin rather than the barbaric medieval tongue and who attacked any form of speculative textual analysis. Textual, especially biblical, commentary should be based solely on uncovering the author's meaning through careful linguistic exegesis founded on a wide knowledge of ancient languages and literature. The first Oxford scholar to evince serious interest in the humanists' campaign was Thomas Chaundler (*c.*1418–1490), warden of New College from 1454 to 1475. Among the next generation, their leading discipline was John Colet (*c.*1467–1519), future dean of St Paul's Cathedral in London, who in 1498 gave private humanist lectures at the university on Paul's Epistle to the Romans. With the foundation of Cardinal College, the new approach received the backing of the leading churchman in the land. Wolsey ordered his new college to teach Latin eloquence and Greek, and the new form of scriptural analysis as well as 'the subtle scholastic questions' of Duns Scotus.[13]

Oxford's interest in producing effective pastors was part of a European-wide campaign to improve the quality of the clergy in the fifteenth century. It was also both a reaction and a response to the university's last great fourteenth-century theologian, John Wyclif (d.1384), who had taught in the 1370s and early 1380s. A number of earlier Oxford philosophers and theologians had stirred controversy but they had kept on the right side of orthodoxy. Wyclif crossed the line by arguing that priests and bishops who did not live holy lives ceased to have any spiritual authority and could have their property revoked by the state. He also claimed that a good layman could preach the truths of Scripture and wanted the Bible to be available in English so all could read it. Wyclif was condemned as a heretic, and from 1412 all heads of halls and colleges had to swear not to admit even a servant 'who may in all likelihood be guilty of heretical ... depravity'.[14] Wyclif, however, had the last laugh. His supporters formed an underground movement in the church which proved impossible to eradicate and was still troubling the authorities when Henry VIII took the momentous decision to break with Rome.

Divinity School, featuring Oxford's finest late perpendicular vaulting; built for the faculty of theology by William Orchard (d.1504), it was completed in 1488. Print from William Combe, *A History of the University of Oxford* (published by Ackermann, 1814).

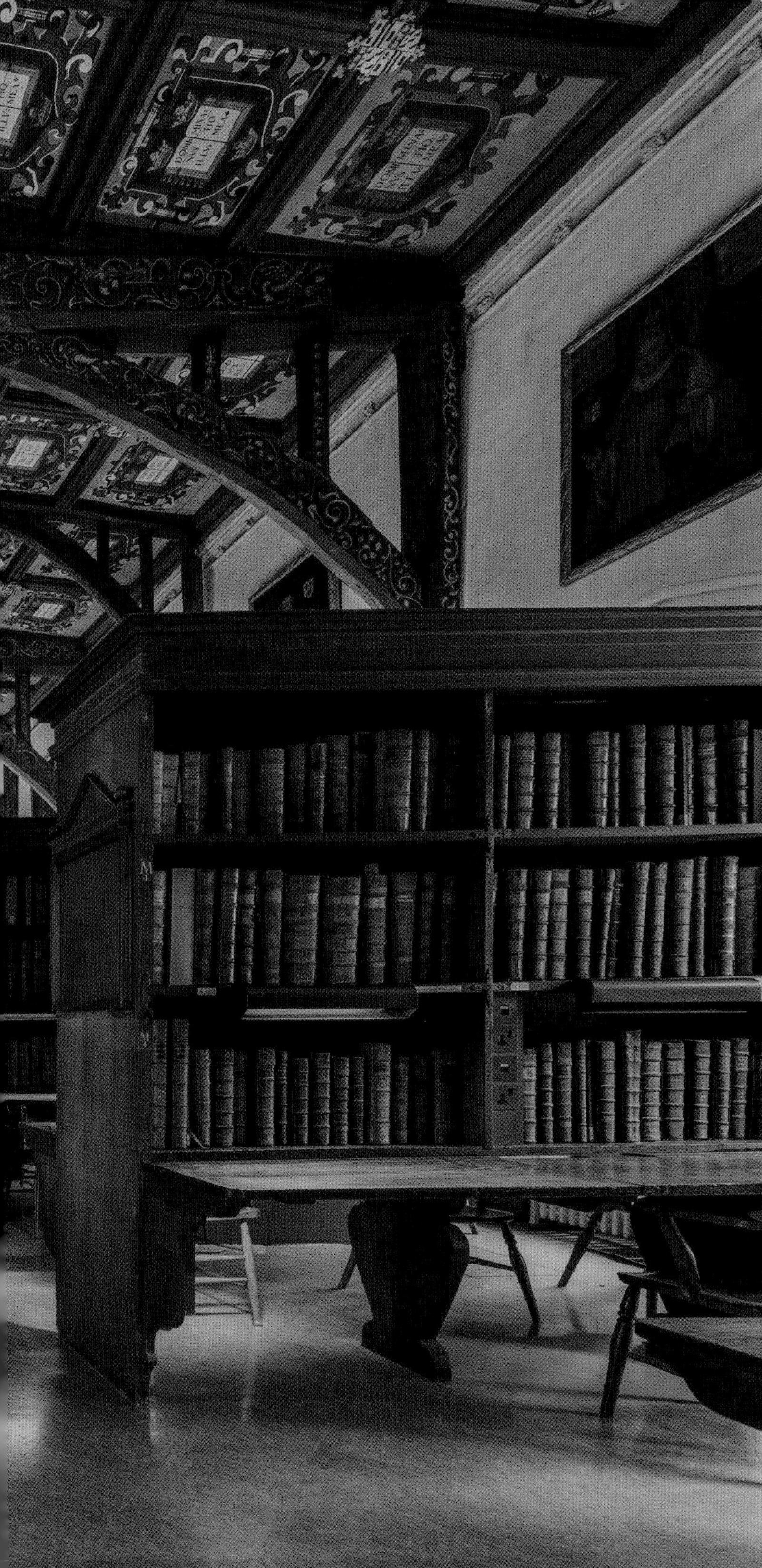

Duke Humfrey's Library, 1488: built above the Divinity School to house the books given to the university by the duke of Gloucester (1391–1447), brother of Henry V.

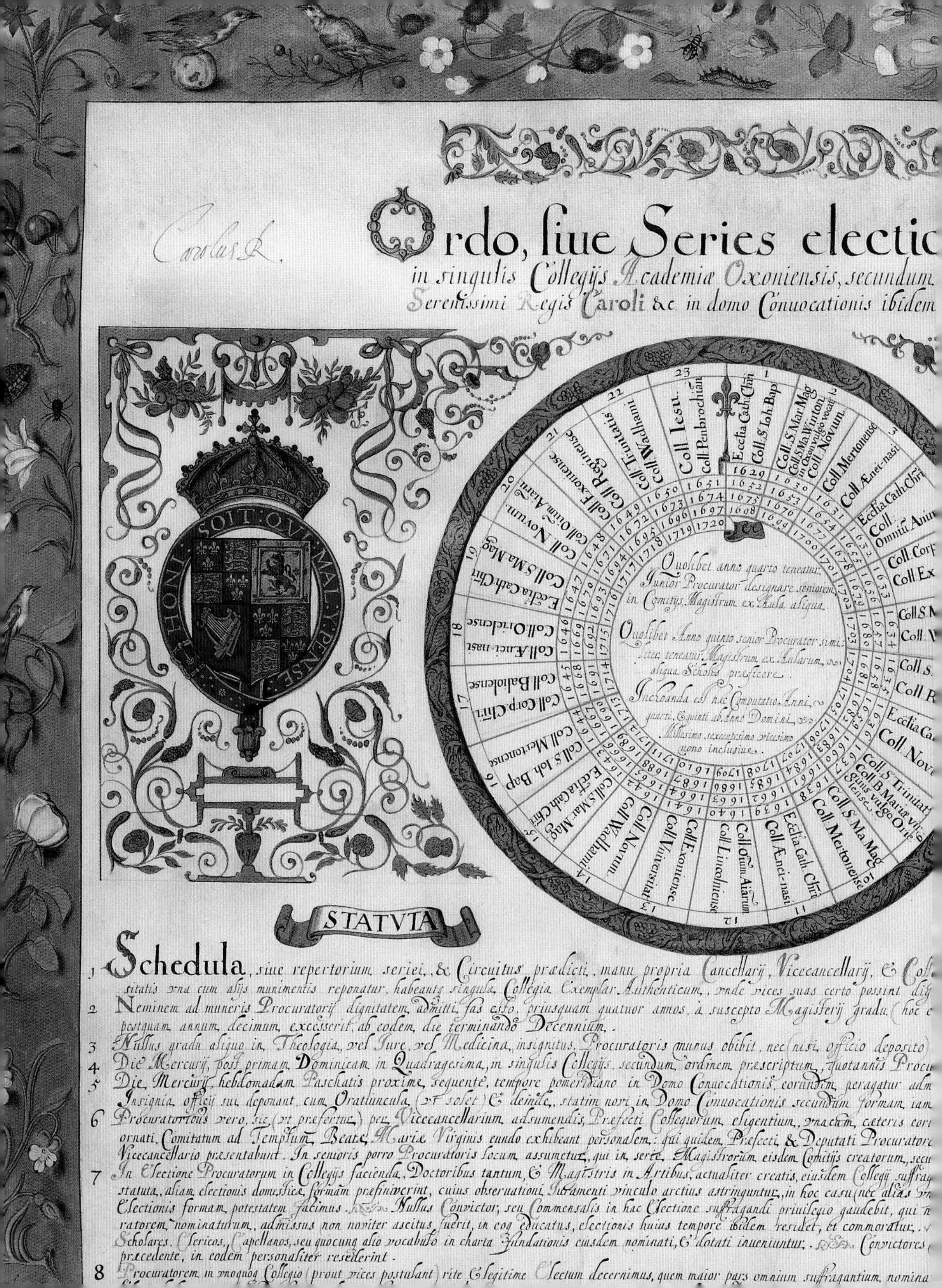

Carolus R.

Ordo, siue Series electio

in singulis Collegijs Academiæ Oxoniensis, secundum
Serenissimi Regis Caroli &c in domo Conuocationis ibidem

Quolibet anno quarto teneatur Iunior Procurator designare seniorem, in Comitijs, Magistrum ex Aula aliqua.

Quolibet Anno quinto senior Procurator similiter teneatur Magistrum ex Aularum aliqua Scholis præficere.

Inchoanda est hæc Computatio Anni quarti, & quinti ab Anno Domini Millesimo sexcentesimo vicesimo nono inclusiue.

STATVTA

1 **Schedula**, siue repertorium seriei, & Circuitus prædicti, manu propria Cancellarij, Vicecancellarij, & Coll
sitatis vna cum alijs munimentis reponatur, habeantq singula Collegia Exemplar Authenticum, vnde vices suas certo possint dig

2 Neminem ad muneris Procuratorij dignitatem admitti fas esto, priusquam quatuor annos, à suscepto Magisterij gradu (hoc e
postquam annum decimum excesserit, ab eodem die terminando Decennium.

3 Nullus gradu aliquo in Theologia, vel Iure, vel Medicina, insignitus, Procuratoris munus obibit, nec (nisi officio deposito)

4 Die Mercurij, post primam Dominicam in Quadragesima, in singulis Collegijs, secundum ordinem præscriptum, quotannis Procu

5 Die Mercurij, hebdomadam Paschatis proxime sequente, tempore pomeridiano in Domo Conuocationis, eorundem peragatur adm
Insignia officij sui deponant, cum Oratiuncula (vt solet) & deinde, statim noui in Domo Conuocationis secundum formam iam

6 Procuratoribus vero, sic (vt præfertur) per Vicecancellarium adsumendis, Præfecti Collegiorum eligentium, vnacum, cæteris cor
ornati, Comitatum ad Templum Beatæ Mariæ Virginis eundo exhibeant personalem: qui quidem Præfecti, & Deputati Procurator
Vicecancellario præsentabunt. In senioris porro Procuratoris locum assumetur, qui in serie Magistrorum eisdem Comitijs creatorum, secu

7 In Electione Procuratorum in Collegijs facienda, Doctoribus tantum, & Magistris in Artibus, actualiter creatis, eiusdem Collegij suffrag
statuta, aliam electionis domesticæ formam præfiniuerint, cuius obseruationi Iuramenti vinculo arctius astringuntur, in hoc casu (nec alias
Electionis formam, potestatem facimus. Nullus Conuictor, seu Commensalis in hac Electione suffragandi priuilegio gaudebit, qui n
ratorem nominaturum, admissus non noviter ascitus fuerit, in eoq educatus, electionis huius tempore ibidem residet, et commoratur.
Scholares, Clericos, Capellanos, seu quocunq alio vocabulo in charta Fundationis eiusdem nominati, & dotati inueniuntur. Conuictores
præcedente, in eodem personaliter resederint.

8 Procuratorem in vnoquoq Collegio (prout vices postulant) rite, & legitime Electum decernimus, quem maior pars omnium suffragantium nomina

The Anglican Seminary

THE REFORMATION AND ITS AFTERMATH

The Protestant Reformation which began in the 1530s was not completed until Henry VIII's daughter Elizabeth was securely on the throne forty years later. In the religious conflict that divided mid Tudor England, the University of Oxford largely supported the old church. Fervent Protestants were to be found in its midst but Cambridge was the stronghold of religious reform. It was for this reason that, during the Marian reaction, Archbishop Thomas Cranmer (1480–1556) was brought to Oxford to be tried for heresy and burnt: there was no chance that he would receive a sympathetic hearing and his execution outside Balliol passed without incident. Even in the first part of Elizabeth's reign, much of Oxford remained religiously conservative. When the queen came to the university in 1566 and attended a disputation, she was particularly impressed by a young fellow of St John's, Edmund Campion (1540–1581), who would later be hanged for treason as a Jesuit. From the mid 1570s, however, in Oxford as in the rest of England, the religious temper changed as a generation reached adulthood who had only known the Church of England. By then there were few members of the university who were not firm supporters of the predestinarian form of Protestantism associated with the Frenchman John Calvin (1509–1564). In 1581 the university passed a statute requiring those coming into residence 'of 16 or upward' to swear that the queen was head of the reformed church and that the Thirty-Nine Articles of 1571, which set out its doctrine, were a true statement of faith.[15] Thereafter until 1854 Oxford was a confessional university. Only Anglicans, or those willing to subscribe to Anglicanism, could attend.

This did not mean that Oxford or the new Anglican Church was monolithic. From the beginning of Elizabeth's reign Oxford harboured a number of Protestant reformers who believed that her religious settlement of 1559 had not gone far enough. Known as Puritans, figures such as president of Corpus Christi John Rainolds (1549–1607) demanded that a simpler form of worship be established along strict Calvinist lines and frequently refused to follow the liturgy laid down in the Book of Common Prayer. The Puritans were always an object of crown suspicion, but they held the moral high ground in the university until the mid 1620s. In the reign of Charles I they were pushed onto the defensive when Oxford's chancellor, Archbishop William Laud (1573–1645), ordered that college communion tables be placed once again altar-wise at the east end and railed off, and several young theologians attacked the doctrine of predestination on the grounds that Christ offered salvation to all. With the king's defeat in the Civil War, the Puritans came into their own again and the national church was reformed along the lines they had desired for so long. Their victory, however, was short-lived. With the restoration of the monarchy in 1660, Elizabeth's church, shorn of its Laudian accretions, returned. The old battle was then once more rejoined, although in a much more muted form as many erstwhile Puritans became dissenters.[16]

There were no more bitter religious disputes in Anglican Oxford until the mid eighteenth century and the furore caused by John Wesley (1703–1791), a fellow of Lincoln in the 1730s and 1740s. Wesley felt that the Church of England of the Age of Enlightenment was headed by rationalist theologians or latitudinarians who merely paid lip service to its doctrines. As a result, the church had lost its earlier evangelical fervour and abandoned the people of England to godlessness. On 24 August 1744 he preached a sermon in St Mary's where he apparently informed his audience that 'there was not one Christian among all the Heads of Houses' and that all the fellows 'were useless to a proverbial uselessness'.[17] Understandably Wesley's diatribe fell

Christ Church Hall, late 1520s: Oxford's largest dining hall in its most famous college, initially set up in 1525 by Cardinal Wolsey, then refounded in 1547 by Henry VIII.

on deaf ears and his supporters in the university were subject to persistent hostility and ridicule. Slowly, however, the number of self-styled evangelicals in Oxford grew, and by the early nineteenth century they formed a formidable phalanx. In the 1830s and 1840s, however, their enemy was no longer simply latitudinarian Anglicans but a new group of ritualists in the university, led by the Oriel fellow John Henry Newman (1801–1890). The Newmanites, or Tractarians as they were called after the tracts they published, went much further than Laud had ever done in promoting 'popish' practices: they crossed themselves, genuflected and even wore stoles. They also insisted that the Anglican Church take a much greater interest in the plight of the poor, which quickly won them support among the students attracted by their idealism. As long as Newman made no attempt to question Anglican doctrine, the sect escaped censure. But in 1841, in Tract 90, Newman argued that the Thirty-Nine Articles could be understood in a Roman Catholic sense, which implied that salvation came through works as well as faith.[18] The evangelicals were scandalized and the gloves were off. Four years later Newman declared his conversion to Rome and retired from the university. Some fifty other Tractarians followed suit.

The Reformation brought changes to the university's governance as well as its religious allegiance. Hitherto, the crown had taken little interest in Oxford's affairs as long as students kept the peace. It had been the church's university, and it was the church that kept a weather eye on what was taught and churchmen who founded the colleges, if laymen occasionally provided extra financial support. The establishment of the monarch as head of the new church made the organization and orthodoxy of England's two universities a state concern. As early as 1535 a royal visitation descended on the university to purge it of its Roman ways: the convents

Burning of the Protestant bishops Hugh Latimer and Nicholas Ridley outside Balliol on 15 October 1555. From John Foxe, *Actes and Monuments* (1563).

OVERLEAF
Bodleian Library and the Schools Quadrangle from the south, 1602–24: the university's heartland ever since, inspired and partly paid for by the diplomat Sir Thomas Bodley (1545–1613). Print from David Loggan, *Oxonia Illustrata* (1675).

Si corpꝰ meū tradam igni
caritatem autē non habeā
nihil vtilitatis &c.
Smith.
Latimer.
Ridley
In manꝰ tuas domine.
Father of heauē receiue
my soule.
M. Ridley I will
member your

BIBLIOTHECA PUBLICA BODLEIANA & SCHOLÆ SIV

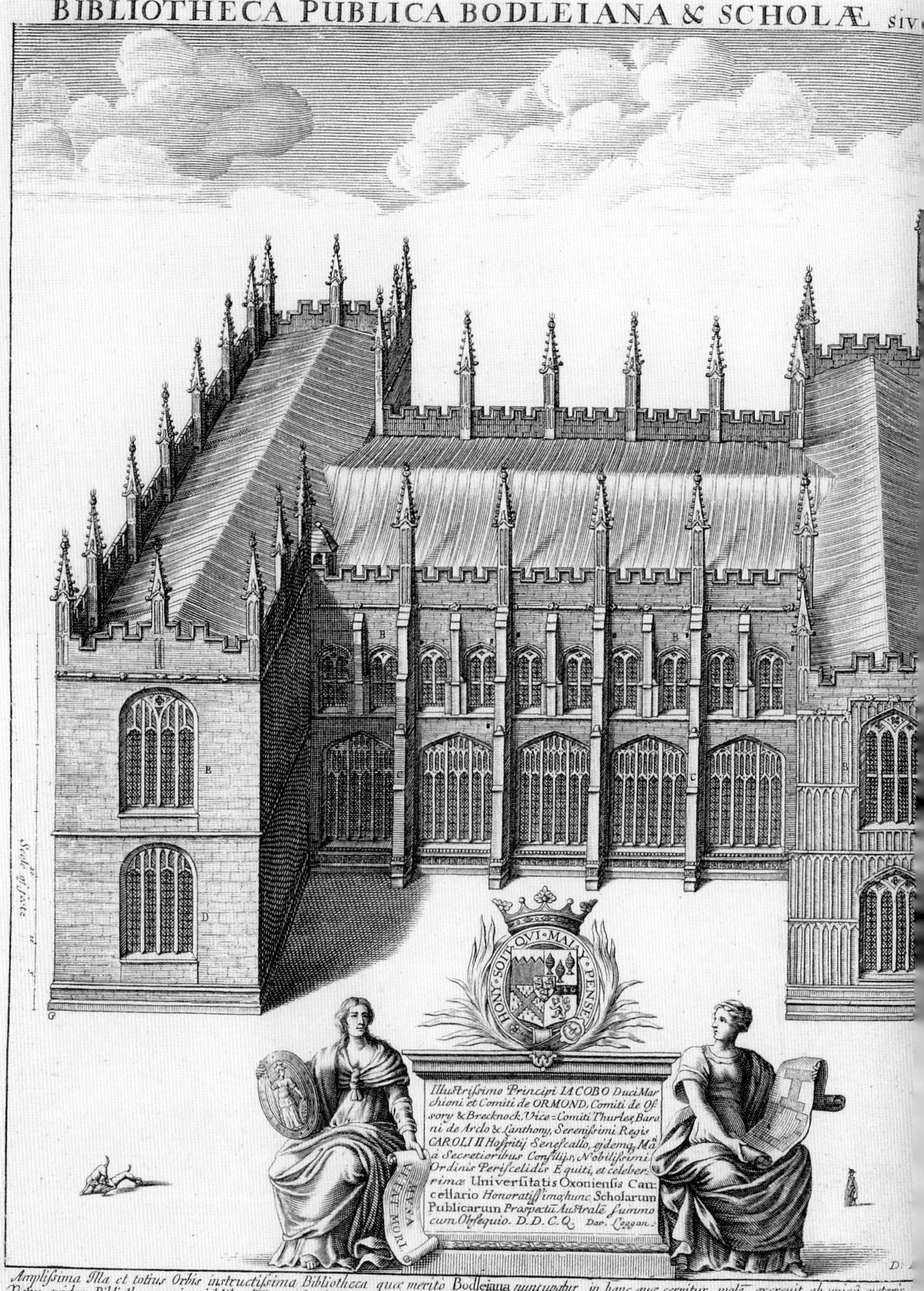
HONY SOIT QVI MAL Y PENSE
Illustrissimo Principi IACOBO Duci Mar
chioni et Comiti de ORMOND, Comiti de Of=
sory & Brecknock, Vice=Comiti Thurles, Baro
ni de Arclo & Lanthony, Serenissimi Regis
CAROLI II Hospitij Senescallo, ejdemq Mā
à Secretioribus Consilijs, Nobilissimi
Ordinis Periscelidis Equiti, et celeber=
rimæ Universitatis Oxoniensis Can=
cellario Honoratissimo, hunc Scholarum
Publicarum Prospectū Australē summo
cum Obsequio. D.D.C.Q. Dav. Loggan.
MORI.
B
C
D

Amplissima Illa et totius Orbis instructissima Bibliotheca quæ meritò Bodlejana nuncupatur in hanc quæ cernitur molē excreuit ab unicâ veteris
Vetus quidem Bibliotheca quicquid libroru̅ possederit acceptu̅ retulit Munificentiæ Humphredi Ducis Glocestrensis, et Joh: Tipetoft Alumni Baliolens
Suos omnes Latinos Bibliothecæ moriens legavit. Postmodu̅ (cùm Temporu̅ virûmq Injuriâ ita vastata fuerat ut libris direptis et Pluteis ac S
Equit. Aur. Qui à Serenissimâ Reginâ Elizabethâ in exteras Provincias sæpius legatus est, et apud fœderatos Belgas in Senatoriu̅
circa Ann. 1600: hocq et sequentibus annis Alij Viri Literis & Nobilitate Illustres vel Libros vel Pecunias numeratas quotidie et affatim supp
recta; adeò ut totius Bibliothecæ Figura tunc Temporis literam T referre videretur. Et Hoc ipso Anno Honoratissimus simul ac Doctissimus Bod
extructa est Turris Quadrata, et Novæ Scholæ sive Auditoria pro Artibus ac Scientijs singulis ad Numeru̅ Duodenarium, duabus Concame
sumptibus superaddita esset concameratio tertia, Quæ per tria Figuræ quadratæ latera ducitur, et tanquam Ambulacrum reficiendi animi
Bibliotheca aucta est Porticu Occidentali, quæ Boream spectat et Austru̅, cujúsq Concameratio inferior Convocationis Domu̅ constituit. Ita
cæteræ omnes Universi Orbis Academiæ non ostendunt. Plurimi sunt quoru̅ Beneficentiâ (uti et annuis Bodleij Reditibus) Supellex Librari
Digbey & Thomas Roe Equites Aurati, Qui maximam vim Antiquoru̅ Numismatum et Codicum M^ss Ingentē Copiam in Bibliothecæ usum
et maxima) Bibliotheca Ipsius partim, partimq Hæredum Benevolentiâ in nostram Bodlejanam concessit.

ITORIA ARTIUM LIBERALIUM, ut ad Austrum Spectantur.

Insignia Tho. Bodlei.

A Scholæ publicæ
B Bibliotheca pub: Bodleiana
C Schola Theologiæ
D Domus Convocationis
E Porticus sive ambulacra
F F pedes 147
G G pedes 144

DOMI NVS ILLV MINA TIO MEA

Insignia Univ. Oxon.

lp. cum privil. S.R.M.

icu, quæ (jam Bibliothecæ mediana) Scholæ sive Auditorio Theologico Antiquo pariter et Ornatissimo superstruitur, et rectà Ortū respicit ac Occasum.
valore 500 Marcarū libros Testamento donavit; Ille verò libras millenariū numerū superantes, Libros item plures quā ducentos dono dedit; Et præterea
Nihil intus præter nudos parietes superesset) Instauratorē habuit virum Honoratissimū perpetuâq Memoria Dignissimū Thomam Bodlejum
s, Mauritio Comiti Dignitate proximus. Hic (inquā) collapsā Bibliothecā integritati restituit, et omnigenâ Librorū Supellectile adornavit,
osthæc an. 1612 dicti Bodley sumptibus ab humo erecta est, et Monumentis Librariis locupletata Porticus Orientalis ad Austrū & Boreā expor-
maximo Literarū dispendio) Fato cessit. Et paulò post, circa Ann. 1616 (variorū Benefactorū collatis Symbolis) ad Bibliothecæ plagā Orientalē
Munificentissimus Bodlejus ulterius apud se designatū Negotiū ita prius comparārat, ut (legatâ ingenti pecuniæ summâ) propriis post mortē
patet, Fundatorū Colleg: Aliorūmq Doctorū virorum. exhibens Effigies plurimas. Postremò circa Ann. 1636 sumptibus Universitatis
Bibliothecæ Figura (præter Scholarū Fabricam) non sit absimilis literæ H. Et hoc modo absoluta est ingentissimæ molis fabrica, qualem
indies augescit: Inter Quos primas facilè obtinent Gul: Laud ArchiEpiscopus Cantuariensis, Gul: Herbert Comes Pembrochianus, Kenelmus
Nec sanè infimo loco accensendus est vir Clarissimus Joh: Seldenus ex Interiori Templo apud Londinātes J C^tus Doctissimus, Cujus Privata (sed

and colleges of the monks and friars were closed, the teaching of canon law or the law of the old church suppressed, a new emphasis placed on teaching Greek, and scholars required to swear to the legality of the new religious order.[19] Thereafter, until the second half of the eighteenth century, the state continually intruded in the university's life. Ever fearful of religious and political disobedience, successive regimes brought new visitations and fresh demands for oaths of loyalty, while the university was periodically leaned on to pass legislation that would promote the current religious agenda. Even colleges were harassed in their day-to-day business, as the crown, its servants and leading nobles demanded that they elect their clients as heads of house or fellows. Disobedience could bring swift retribution. When the president of Magdalen died in 1687, the Catholic James II ordered the fellows to elect the bishop of Oxford as their head. The fellows, hostile to the bishop's readiness to support the king's policy of tolerating his co-religionists, refused. James was incandescent and declared he had been 'affronted & abus'd more than ever K[ing] was' and would have his 'honour vindicated'. A commission was immediately dispatched to the college and all but three of the fellows were summarily ejected.[20]

The state's desire to keep the university under its thumb also explains a significant adjustment to its formal organization from Elizabeth's reign. On the surface nothing altered. The university continued to be run by the vice-chancellor and proctors, and the masters in Convocation and Congregation took the decisions. But the masters' powers were steadily eroded. Starting in 1569, on the instruction of the chancellor and the queen's favourite the earl of Leicester (*c.*1522–1588), they lost the right to initiate business. Instead, this was entrusted to a small council, eventually called the Hebdomadal Board, which from 1634 comprised the vice-chancellor, proctors and heads

Dorothy Wadham (1534–1618), co-founder with her husband of Wadham College in 1610, the first college to have a hall screen dividing the diners from the servants and kitchen staff. Portrait by William Sonmans, c.1670.

ROTHEA WADHAM NICOLAI CONIVX, DNI GVL. PETRÆI (QVI HENR. VIII^VO, EDV. VI^TO, E
RIÆ AC ELIZABETHÆ REGINIS QVONDAM À SECRETIS FVIT) FILIA, DEMANDATAM

Merton Old Library, 1589–90: Oxford's first stall library, the gift of the college's warden, Sir Henry Savile, who with other Oxford scholars also played a leading part in the creation of the King James Bible (1611).

Ordo, siue Series electionis Procuratorum,

in singulis Collegijs Academiæ Oxoniensis, secundum vices infra scriptas, per statuta Serenissimi Regis Caroli &c in domo Conuocationis ibidem stabilita, & confirmata & quotannis faciendæ.

STATVTA — STATVTA

1 **Schedula**, siue repertorium seriei, & Circuitus prædicti, manu propria Cancellarij, Vicecancellarij, & Collegij cuiusq et Aulæ Præfecti consignata, in Archiuis Vniuersitatis vna cum alijs munimentis reponatur, habeantq singula Collegia Exemplar Authenticum, vnde vices suas certo possint dignoscere.

2 Neminem ad muneris Procuratorij dignitatem admitti fas esto, priusquam quatuor annos, à suscepto Magisterij gradu (hoc est a die creationis suæ in Comitijs publicis) compleuerit, vel postquam annum decimum excesserit ab eodem die terminando Decennium.

3 Nullus gradu aliquo in Theologia, vel Iure vel Medicina insignitus, Procuratoris munus obibit, nec (nisi officio deposito) ad gradum aliquem Procurator quiuis eodem anno promoueatur.

4 Die Mercurij post primam Dominicam in Quadragesima, in singulis Collegijs, secundum ordinem præscriptum, quotannis Procuratorum fiat electio.

5 Die Mercurij, hebdomadam Paschatis proxime sequente, tempore pomeridiano in Domo Conuocationis, eorundem peragatur admissio, quibus loco & tempore, Procuratores anni superioris Insignia officij sui deponant, cum Oratiuncula (vt solet) & deinde, statim noui in Domo Conuocationis secundum formam iam olim vsitatam, per Vicecancellarium admittantur.

6 Procuratoribus vero, sic (vt præfertur) per Vicecancellarium adsumendis, Præfecti Collegiorum eligentium, vnacum cæteris eorundem Alumnis, singuli Ornamentis gradui suo competentibus, ornati, Comitatum ad Templum Beatæ Mariæ Virginis eundo exhibeant personalem: qui quidem Præfecti & Deputati Procuratores respectiue suos, secundum ritum antiquum, admittendos Vicecancellario præsentabunt. In senioris porro Procuratoris locum assumetur, qui in serie Magistrorum eisdem Comitijs creatorum, secundum dispositionem Procuratorum (vti moris est) ordine prior collocatur.

7 In Electione Procuratorum in Collegijs facienda, Doctoribus tantum, & Magistris in Artibus, actualiter creatis, eiusdem Collegij suffragandi ius competat. Quod si priuata cuiusuis Collegij statuta, aliam electionis domesticæ formam præfiniuerint, cuius obseruationi Iuramenti vinculo arctius astringuntur, in hoc casu (nec alias vnquam) ad euitandum periurij periculum, præscriptam immutandi Electionis formam, potestatem facimus. Nullus Conuictor, seu Commensalis in hac Electione suffragandi priuilegio gaudebit, qui non à primo ad Academiam aduentu in Collegium ea vice Procuratorem nominaturum, admissus non nuper ascitus fuerit, in eoq educatus, electionis huius tempore ibidem residet, et commoratur. Residentes vero interpretamur, omnes Collegiorum Socios, Scholares, Clericos, Capellanos, seu quocunq alio vocabulo in charta Fundationis eiusdem nominati, & dotati inueniuntur. Conuictores non item, nisi per sex menses in anno electionem huiusmodi immediate præcedente, in eodem personaliter resederint.

8 Procuratorem in vnoquoq Collegio (prout vices postulant) rite & legitime Electum decernimus, quem maior pars omnium suffragantium nominabit, quod si duo, pari vtriusq numero suffragiorum, nominentur, ille pro Electo habeatur, quem Præfectus vel eo absente seu sede vacante eius vicem gerens nominabit. Sin plures nominentur, nec vnus aliquis maiorem partem suffragiorum omnium retulerit, nec eodem die, eam ob causam, Electio absoluta fuerit, & ante horam nonam vespertinam Vicecancellario renuntiata, Collegium istud ius præsentandi, ista vice amittat, & ad Vicecancellarium spectabit nominatio, qui intra biduum aptam personam, & secundum conditiones superius assignatas, habilem, ex Aularum aliqua desumendam, in Procuratorem cooptabit.

9 Si nullus in Collegio Procuratorem designaturo, habilis reperiatur, qui possit & velit istud munus subire, tunc Collegij istius Præfectus, vel (eo absente aut sede vacante) eius vicem gerens, die Electionis constituto, alium (quem voluerit) habilem in Aularum aliqua degentem nominabit, qui deinde in Procuratorem assumetur.

10 Si Procuratorem aliquem mori contigerit, vel quauis de causa ante anni sui expirationem officio suo cedere, locum eius supplebit alius eiusdem Collegij habilis, & idoneus, per Præfectum, seu (eo absente aut sede vacante) eius vicem gerentem intra septimanam post mortem nominandus. Quod si talis non extiterit, tunc Vicecancellarius, aliquem habilem in Aularum quacunq commorantem, in Procuratorem substituet, vt supra.

11 Nemini Procuratoris absentis vices, ad quamcunq muneris istius expeditionem supplere licebit, qui tres annos à suscepto Magisterij gradu non compleuerit.

12 Vt etiam Aularum quæ in Procuratorum nominatione nullas vices obtinent ratio aliqua habeatur, Volumus, vt quolibet quarto anno, qui Procuratoris iunioris locum sortitur, seniorem in Comitijs eiusdem anni Magistrum Aulæ alicuius Alumnum designet. Procurator vero senior quolibet quinquennio, Magistrum etiam in Aularum aliqua degentem scrolis præficiat.

13 Vt etiam tumultuatio ista, & molestiæ circa Electionem Collectorum Quadragesimalium penitus tollantur, Statuimus, quod Procuratores pro tempore existentes, in Festo Omnium Sanctorum Collectores antedictos designabunt singuli vnum, quem visum fuerit in Collegio quocunq vel Aula degentem. Quorum admissio modo et forma per Domum Conuocationis assignanda celebrabitur. Et, nisi ad alterum ratione promotionis (secundum Statuta Vniuersitatis) Senioritatis ius pertinuerit, qui prius ad gradum Baccalaurei in Artibus præsentatus, et admissus fuerit, Senioris locum occupabit. Atq hi Collectores, Classes Determinantium in Quadragesima, & cætera, quæ secundum morem antiquum sui muneris sunt, præstituent, & ordinabunt: Si vero Procurator, quiuis, circa Collationem officij Collectoris prædicti, pretij accepti, seu repetundarum, conuictus fuerit, idem eo ipso officio suo submouebitur. & feuda quæcunq, seu pecuniarum summas, a Baccalaureis eiusdem anni, per eum acceptas, in vsum Cistæ Academicæ, præsentis Statuti vigore Vicecancellario refundere tenebitur.

14 Si ambiguitas aliqua, vel dubium aliquod præter prænominata occurrat, circa Electionem modo præfinito in Collegijs faciendam, ne, aliscente inter partes discordia, scandalum exinde oriatur, per Vicecancellarium Doctorem in Theologia seniorem (modo sit præfectus Collegij alicuius) tempore Electionis Domi præsentem, & Præfectum Collegij in Electione tunc temporis interesse habentem, vel horum duos (quorum Collegij Præfectum vnum esse volumus) controuersia istiusmodi terminetur. Quod si Præfectus Collegij antedictus tunc temporis Vicecancellarij locum obtinuerit, tunc duos in Theologia Doctores, maxime seniores (sed Collegiorum vt præfertur Præfectos) sibi assumat, quibuscum causæ istius cognitionem habeat.

Atq hæc Statuta, singulasq eorundem particulas, nulli Dispensationi quauis de causa sub prætextu quouismodo, obnoxia, perpetuo inuiolata manere volumus.

The Proctorial Cycle, 1628: calendar organizing the order in which the colleges would elect from their ranks the university's chief disciplinary officers.

of house. The proctors too were no longer elected annually from the body of masters and doctors but after 1628 from the graduate fellows of two colleges in turn according to a stipulated cycle.[21] Thereby Convocation and Congregation were effectively corralled and Oxford came under the control of the college heads, who themselves were often royal nominees. The masters, however, never totally lost their independence. They continued to elect the chancellor, and in 1604 they gained the right to elect two Members of Parliament (MPs). In the Hanoverian era they used their powers to discomfort the university establishment on many occasions. In 1829 the government of the day finally decided to end discrimination against Roman Catholics by allowing them to sit in Parliament and hold government office. Most Oxford masters were bitterly opposed to the move, and when Sir Robert Peel (1788–1850), one of the university's MPs and a supporter of Catholic Emancipation, put himself forward for re-election he was rejected at the poll.[22]

External interest in the university's affairs was not always a negative force. Before the 1530s Oxford had had to rely on regent masters to maintain the curriculum. A hundred years later, teaching in the four surviving faculties was principally supplied by permanent professors whose chairs had been funded by lay benefactors. In 1540 Henry VIII endowed chairs in Greek, Hebrew, theology, civil law and medicine. It took time for others to follow his example, but in the 1610s and 1620s there was a flurry of new foundations which allowed the university to cover most parts of the traditional arts course and to end the obligation of novice masters to teach. After 1750, moreover, the university was given chairs to support all manner of new disciplines too, especially in the sciences. Between 1810 and 1840, professorships or readerships were created in chemistry, experimental philosophy, mineralogy,

GLORIÆ DEI OPT. MAX
HONORI CAROLI REGIS
IN USUM ACAD. & REIPUB
HENRICUS
COMES
DANBY
DD. MDCXXXII

Danby Gate, 1632–3: entrance to Oxford's Botanic Garden, founded by Henry Danvers, Earl of Danby (1573–1644), in 1621, and here depicted with its first superintendent, Jacob Bobart the elder. From Abel Evans, *Vertumnus* (1713).

geology and rural economy, two of the five thanks to the Prince Regent. True, some of the professors were not always assiduous in performing their functions and pluralism was not unknown. But this was hardly the fault of the laymen whose generosity had provided Oxford by the mid nineteenth century with a large professional professoriate that was the envy of most continental universities.

NUMBERS

The post-Reformation university, like its medieval predecessor, principally existed to provide the church with an educated clergy. From the mid sixteenth century, however, England's lay elites began to be won to the view promoted by Renaissance humanists, such as Erasmus of Rotterdam (1466–1536), that a gentleman as much as a cleric needed a knowledge of classical literature, rhetoric and philosophy. In Elizabeth's reign Oxford started to welcome a new clientele as students intended for lay professions, administrative office or a life of leisure on the family estate came to the university. As a result, numbers rose. In 1552, when the successful establishment of the Reformation was still in doubt, there were not many more than 1,000 students and masters at Oxford.[23] Thereafter the number expanded sharply. The university kept a matriculation register from 1565, and in that year admitted 250 students. By the 1630s this figure had risen to 460, and a university census in 1634 recorded 3,305 scholars in residence.[24]

From the late seventeenth century, however, attendance began to contract again. New views about a gentleman's education, propounded by John Locke (1603–1704), among others, stressed the need for the young to learn modern languages, history and geography, and the art of pleasing. Too long a stay at a university bred a pedant. The non-clerical clientele therefore declined. So too did the number of students from poorer backgrounds. Prior to the Civil War, sons of merchants and yeomen had swarmed to Oxford and Cambridge in the hope of finding a place in the church. But from 1660 England's parishes were staffed with the younger sons of the landed gentry and opportunities for the poor were greatly reduced. By the 1750s matriculations were down to 200 a year. They picked up again at the turn of the nineteenth century when the horrors of the French Revolution convinced the elite that its sons needed a good dose of college discipline and the classics to keep them clear of radicalism. And by the 1820s, although the poor students had not returned in any numbers, the annual intake had risen to 364. But even in 1850 the university was still only half the size it had been two centuries before. In 1842 a head count of undergraduates or students yet to take their Bachelor of Arts (BA) revealed there were only 1,200 in residence.[25]

Laudian Code, 1636: compilation and rationalization of Oxford's statutes from the mid thirteenth century, presided over by its chancellor, Archbishop Laud.

The university's failure in the first half of the nineteenth century to return to the heyday of the 1630s reflected in part a collapse in numbers staying beyond the four years needed to qualify for a BA. In the first part of the seventeenth century up to half the university may have been long-term residents. In 1850 there were no more than 550 older students on the books, all college fellows, many of whom were not involved in serious study or even present. Magdalen had a fellowship of forty; in 1836 the number in the college at any time hovered between nine and seventeen.[26] This reflected in turn the continued unimportance of professional qualifications in England. In other Protestant states ministers of religion needed a theology degree, and in most Continental countries lawyers and physicians eventually required a degree in law and medicine. But this was never the case in premodern England, where even Anglican ministers only had to have a BA. In the first flush

TIT. XIV. DE VESTITV ET HABITV SCHOLASTICO.

§. 1. De Vestitu Præfectorum, Sociorum & Scholarium Collegiorum; Et de modo in Vestibus seruando a cæteris.

STATVTVM est, quod [1] omnes Præfecti, Collegiorum Socij et 1) B. 111. b.
Scholares, necnon omnes Sacris Ordinibus initiati, prout Clericos decet,
vestiantur; et ea obseruent, quæ Canonicis sanctionibus præcipiuntur.

Quodque alij omnes (exceptis filijs Baronum in Superiore Parliamenti
Domo suffragij ius habentium) vestibus coloris nigri [2] aut subfusci se assuefaciant; nec 2) KK. 5. b.
quæ fastum aut luxum præ se ferunt, imitentur; sed ab ijs procul absint.

Insuper ab absurdo illo et fastuoso, publice in [3] ocreis ambulandi more abstinere 3) N. 156. b.
compellantur.

Etiam in capillitio modus esto; nec cincinnos, aut comam nimis promissam alant.

Si quis vero in præmissis deliquerit, si Graduatus fuerit, pœnâ 6^s et 8^d plectatur, toties quoties. Si non Graduatus (si per ætatem conveniat) pœnâ corporali; sin minus, arbitrio Vice-cancellarij vel Procuratorum (ita vt summam præfatam non excedant) coërceatur. Quas mulctas, partim ad Vniuersitatis, partim ad proprios vsus exigendi, Procuratores potestatem habeant.

§. 2. De reprimendis et puniendis novos et insolitos Habitus invehentibus.

STATVTVM est, quod, si contingat, aliquos, in vestitu novos et insolitos Habitus introducere, Viceccancellarius, et Præfecti Collegiorum et Aularum, habita inter se deliberatione, de eodem sententias suas in medium proferant.

Deinde Viceccancellarius Scissoribus siue Sartoribus vestiarijs, huiusmodi vestes conficiendi potestate interdicat; et Præfecti suis singuli Scholaribus huiusmodi vestimentorum vsu interdicant.

Si maius remedio vitium invaluerit, nec pœnis, quamvis seueris (quas secundum qualitatem delicti pro arbitrio infliget Viceccancellarius) morbi pertinacia expugnari possit, post tres monitiones, vel pœnas ordinarias ter inflictas ad Bannitionem procedere licebit.

§. 3. Habitus Academici, singulis Gradibus et Facultatibus competentes.

STATVTVM [1] est, quod non graduati, quotquot alicuius Collegij Socij, Pro- 1) B. 119. & 120.
bationarij, Scholares, Capellani, Clerici, Choristæ, denique quotquot de Fundatione Collegij cuiusuis fuerint, Studentes insuper Ædis Christi, quoties in publicum in Vniuersitate prodeunt, Togis laxè manicatis, et Pileis quadratis induti incedent.

Quotquot

of the new world of the Reformation there may have been enthusiasm among aspirant clerics to gain theological training at university. However, after 1660 it died from a lack of encouragement, especially as there was no reduction in the long years it took to gain a degree in the subject. Many new chairs were founded in the three higher faculties after 1750 but this did nothing to enhance their appeal. The faculty of civil law had a chair in common law from 1755 but this did not attract students at the London Inns of Court to Oxford: it was mostly undergraduates who attended the lectures.

The fact that only entrants to the ministry ever needed a degree meant that there were always students who left before they took their BA, let alone completed their arts course. In the seventeenth and eighteenth centuries this was usually half the intake. Presumably many young gentlemen merely stayed for a couple of years and treated the university as a finishing school. In the first half of the nineteenth century the drop-out rate declined to a quarter after the university found a way of stimulating their interest. Under the university's revised statutes of 1636, known as the Laudian Code, the arts course had continued to be split in two: qualification for the BA required a four-year study of Latin and Greek grammar and rhetoric, logic, ethics and geometry; qualification for the MA required a further three years, principally of the study of metaphysics, natural philosophy, and higher and practical mathematics.[27] The proficiency of the candidates for either degree was never rigorously tested, and dispensations were readily available for those unwilling to jump through the stipulated hoops. New university statutes passed in 1800 and 1807 maintained the BA as a four-year course but expanded its content to include the material hitherto studied for the Master's degree. At the same time, the degree was awarded only after success in a new and more demanding oral examination. Weak students could gain

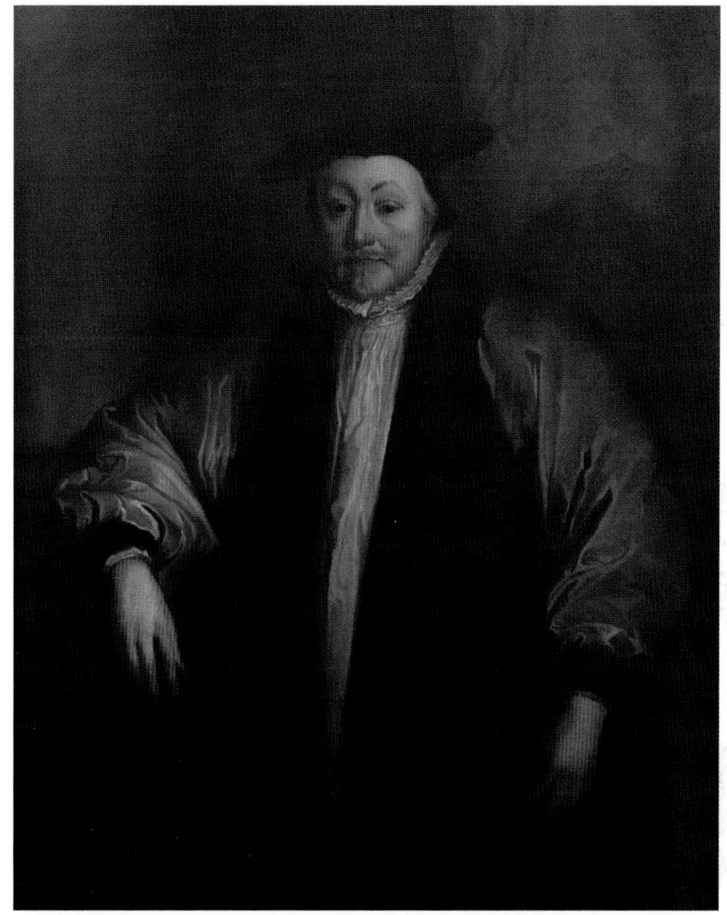

William Laud (1573–1645), Archbishop of Canterbury, chancellor of Oxford (1630–41) and university benefactor. Portrait after Van Dyck, c.1670.

a BA simply by being quizzed on a small number of classical texts of their own choosing. Their more ambitious brethren could offer as many texts as they liked, undergo an examination in physics and mathematics as well as classical literature and philosophy, and opt in either case to be ranked in one of two classes.[28] The new competitive examination was immediately popular. So many students sought the 'honour' of being ranked that, from 1830, the number of classes was extended to four. But the examination was also extremely time-consuming. When

[C]oll[ected] Michaelmas Terme in Dr Hoods time
Oct. 26. 1660.

Edvardus Stradling Baronettus — 1 — 06 — 08
Guil. Price pl. f. — 0 — 02 — 06
Owen Prichard Jdem — 0 — 00 — 00

1 — 09 — 02

Hilary Terme Mar. 16. 1660

[R]ich. Philipps an. 17. f. Howel P. de Dolekaidd, Caermarth Gen. 0 — 05 — 00
[T]ho. Marrys an. 16. f. Rice M. de Hereford Sacerdotis — 0 — 02 — 06
[R]ich. Stokes f. Anth. St. de Rock Com. Pembr. pleb. — 0 — 02 — 06
Howel Thomas f. Ric. Thomas de Pitcott Glamorg. pleb. 0 — 02 — 06
[T]ho. ffranklyn f. Th. ffr. de Caermarth plebeii — 0 — 02 — 06
[R]ob. ffoulkes f. Rice ff. de Llanbykangel, Radnor. min — 0 — 02 — 06
Mar. 22.
Tho. Williams an. 20. f. Guil. W. de S. Nicholas Glamorg. pl. 0 — 02 — 06
10.

1 — 00 — 00

Easter Terme Mai. 17. 1661

[H]arbert Rickards an. 18. fil. Rob. R. de Bridgnorth Salop pl. 0 — 02 — 06
[E]van Anwill an. 17. f. Guil. A. de Dolgelley Merion pp. — 0 — 00 — 00
[ ]t Joh. Jones Gen. 0 — 05 — 00
[ ]Maur. Williams Min. 0 — 05 — 06

12 — 06

Trinity Terme. 1661 Jul. 12.

David Richard an. 20. f. Ric. David de Llanonen Cardig. pl. — 0 — 02 — 06
Jul. 19
Rice Williams an. 15. f. Ric. W. de Rydodin Caerm. Armi — 0 — 10 — 00
Car. Walbiffe an. 15. fil. Car. W. de Llankamlock Brecon. Arm. 0 — 10 — 00
Joh. Wynne an. 17. f. Rob. W. de Nergwis fflint Genri — 0 — 05 — 00
[H]an. Williams an. 18. f. Joh. W. de Penpont Brecon. Mini — 0 — 05 — 00
Edw. Jones an. 21. fil. Joh. Thomas de Nergwis fflint ppris — 0 — 00 — 00
Jul. 20.
Tho. Rees an. 17 f. Th. R. de St Brides major Glam. Genri — 0 — 05 — 00
21.

1 — 17 — 06

The whole year 4 — 19 — 02

Hen. Mich.
Geor. Sto
1661 H
[Ja]n. 15. God
filing
Japun
[Fe]b. 24. Edw. W.
Rob. Por
Phil. H
Dav. L
Joh. W
Michae
Saules W.
Morgan
10.
Henr.
Leolin
Mai. East
Mauri
Jun. Tri
Humphr
Joh. O
Joh. Jo
Guil.
Petr.
Rob.

University matriculation register: a list by college, begun in 1565, of the students in a given year who took the loyalty oath and paid the matriculation fee; depicted here is the list of students from Jesus College in 1660–62.

the philosopher Sir William Hamilton (1788–1856) presented himself to the examiners in 1810, it took two days to question him on all the books he offered for the humane literature exam. The solution from the mid 1820s was to replace the oral exam for the most part with a printed question paper.

The significant proportion of gentlemen's sons that the university educated over the period – even if their number fell in the eighteenth century and many did not take their studies very seriously – turned early modern Oxford into a training ground for the state as well as the church. The crown had frequently poached Oxford's best graduates for state service in the Late Middle Ages. As some of the lay students of gentry and noble stock who flooded into the university after the Reformation found their way to court, the crown continued to draw many of its servants from Oxford in an age when it was no longer acceptable for bishops to hold high secular office. Sir Walter Raleigh (?1552–1618), an Oriel alumnus, was a typical example in the Elizabethan era. After 1660 the Oxonian presence at the heart of government only grew. In the late sixteenth and first half of the seventeenth century, the Oxford-educated gentry who lived on their estates had been involved in central government only when they infrequently represented their local community as MPs. After the Civil War, when England became a parliamentary monarchy and Parliament began to meet each year, many of them became permanently installed at Westminster and the most able and ambitious rose to be ministers of the crown, as Oxford students have continued to do ever since. Oxford never had a monopoly in this regard. Cambridge after 1550 saw a similar laicization of its clientele, and its gentry alumni similarly sought preferment at court and later competed for posts in the cabinet. But Oxford from the mid eighteenth century enjoyed the lion's share of the ministerial spoils. The country's first prime minister, Sir Robert

Walpole, was a Cambridge man, but most of his successors were Oxonians, including the two giants of the nineteenth century, Sir Robert Peel (1788–1850), and William Gladstone (1809–1898), both educated at Christ Church in the years following the implementation of the new examination statute. Both took a first.

COLLEGES AND TUTORS

Between the Henrician Reformation and the outbreak of the English Civil War, six further colleges were founded at Oxford. The first was established by the king himself, who in 1546 set up Christ Church on the site of Wolsey's Cardinal College, whose wealth and property Henry had seized when his chief minister fell from grace. Christ Church was even grander than its predecessor: its chapel was the diocesan church of the new diocese of Oxford, and its income of £2,000 a year supported the dean and chapter as well as 100 fellows and scholars.[29] The other five colleges were set up by a mix of merchants and gentry and a cathedral prebend, who endowed the university with more modest gifts. Trinity and St John's were founded in 1555, Jesus (for Welsh students) in 1571, and Wadham and Pembroke in 1610 and 1624. Thereafter there were no new foundations until the late nineteenth century, apart from Worcester in 1714, and Hertford in 1740, which failed to survive and was dissolved in 1814.

As attendance at the university was expanding fast after 1550, the colleges and the surviving halls had no difficulty in attracting paying boarders. The problem was rather where to put them. In Elizabeth's reign, rooms were subdivided and students crammed into attics, but colleges quickly ran out of space. From the late sixteenth century, with Merton leading the way, overcrowding was solved by constructing additional quadrangles. By 1640 virtually every college had put up new buildings either through seeking funds from former alumni or by taking advantage of rising rents to finance improvement from their endowments. From the late seventeenth century, once numbers fell, the pressure on accommodation declined. That colleges continued to put up new buildings in the eighteenth and early nineteenth centuries was the result of changes in fashion and clientele. In the first half of the seventeenth century, the colleges were built in Renaissance Gothic, the mixed late Perpendicular and classical style much in favour in late Elizabethan and early Stuart England. By the eighteenth century fellows and well-to-do commoners[30] only wanted to live in classical buildings where the rooms were spacious and airy. This meant either putting up further buildings on the existing site, like Christ Church's Peckwater and Canterbury quads (1706–10 and 1775), or pulling down what was already there and building afresh, as Queen's did between 1710 and 1760. The surviving halls, of course, were not so well placed to adjust to the changing tastes. Their numbers held up until 1640, but they attracted few students after 1700 and some went out of business. By 1842 their share of the undergraduates was down to 10 per cent.

In 1550 the colleges were primarily residential institutions. A hundred years later their role had extended to teaching the BA curriculum. In the Late Middle Ages students at all levels had attended lectures in the faculties' schools. There was no provision for formal teaching in-house before Magdalen was empowered by its statutes to appoint stipendiary lecturers in theology and philosophy.[31] A hundred years later most colleges provided public lectures in Greek, rhetoric, logic and ethics, and a handful in Hebrew and mathematics, with the result that the university's professors in these subjects were free to concentrate on the more abstruse or novel aspects of their

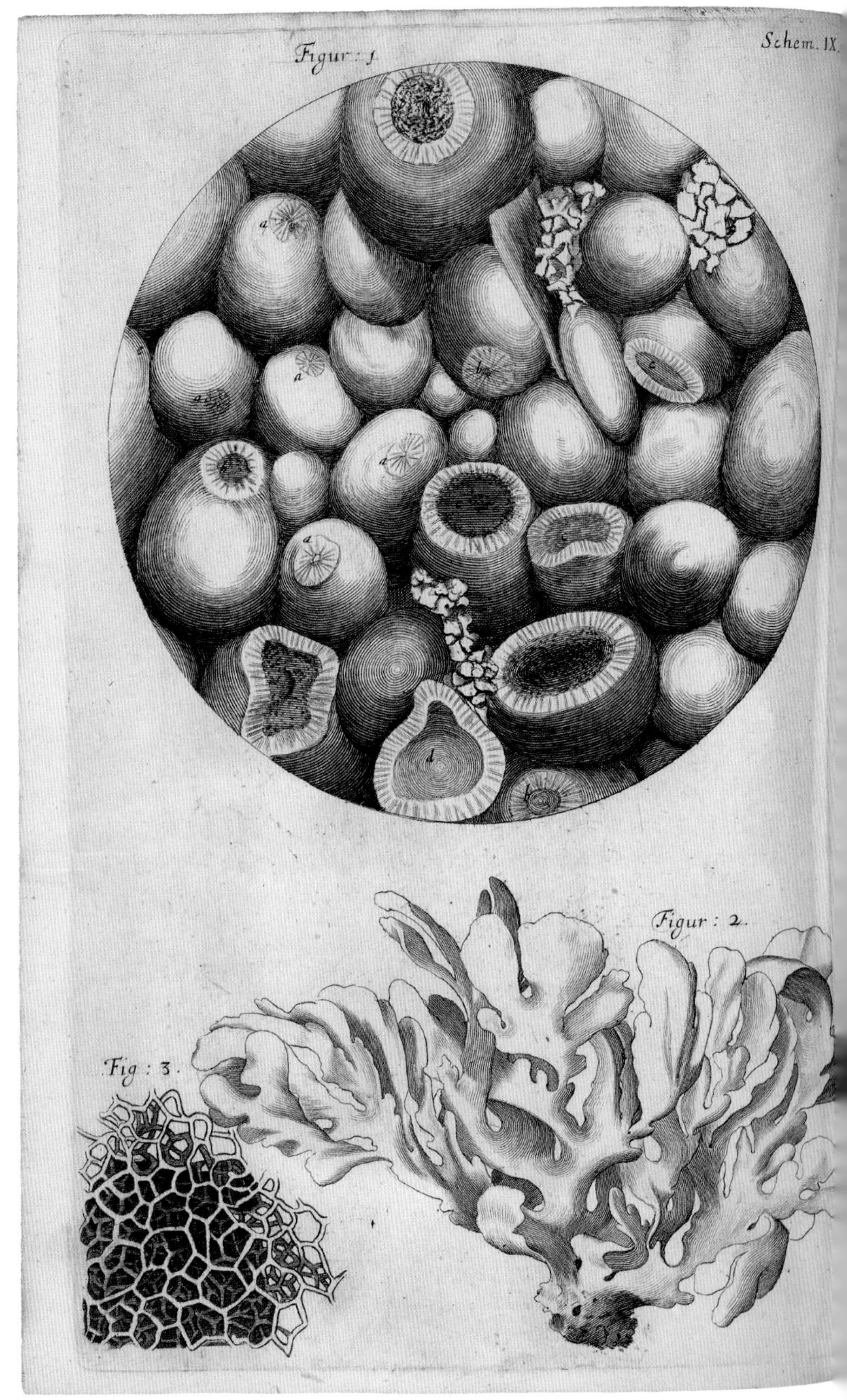
Figur: 1
Figur: 2.
Fig: 3.

Microscopic view of kettering stone from *Micrographia* (1665), a pioneering work by Robert Hooke (1635–1703), one of the leading members of the mid-seventeenth-century Oxford society of experimental philosophers.

discipline. By then too both the colleges and the halls also kept a close watch over the progress of the undergraduates in their midst through the development of the tutorial system. While the colleges quickly saw the material value of admitting paying boarders, they recognized that unsupervised guests could be more trouble than they were worth. From the beginning, therefore, they insisted that each commoner should have a tutor, usually one of the fellowship, who would stand as guarantor for any debts the student might incur and keep the undergraduate on a tight leash. From about 1600 tutors took on an active educational role as well, and began to advise their charges on the books they should read in addition to attending college or university lectures. Fifty years later, they were fully fledged teachers, offering their indifferently prepared pupils elementary instruction in the key parts of the course before they began formal study. Indeed, by the mid eighteenth century the tutor's classes were often the only ones an undergraduate attended in college and the official lecturers were stood down. College lectures in most cases were revived only in the first half of the nineteenth century when, to save duplication, the duties were shared out among the tutors.

The tutors provided their services for a fee, which enhanced the income they received as fellows.[32] Until 1700 they were engaged directly by an undergraduate's parents but thereafter the heads of house took control of the system and selected a small number of fellows in whom they had confidence to act as official tutors. The dedication and ability of some tutors were extremely high. They met frequently with their pupils for study, often twice a day, accompanied them on excursions in the countryside and got to know them as individuals. The most assiduous thought carefully about their teaching and fostered an interactive approach to learning. A large part of a three-hour class with Obadiah Walker (1616–1699) at University College in the early 1670s was given over to 'the Scholars *conferring* with one another in circles, ... and disputing on questions given them the reading before'.[33] Only the last hour was devoted to a new topic. But not all tutors were steadfast. The historian Edward Gibbon (1737–1794) went up to Magdalen in 1752. His tutor, Thomas Winchester (1712–1780), did nothing for his money. 'Instead of guiding the studies, and watching over the behaviour of his disciple, I was never summoned to attend even the ceremony of a lecture.'[34]

Old Ashmolean, 1683: built to house the collection of antiquities and natural history left to the university by Elias Ashmole (1617–1692), possibly designed by Sir Christopher Wren. From Anthony Wood, *The History and Antiquities of the Colleges and Halls*, ed. J. Gutch (1786–90).

Tutors had to cope with students of very different abilities. The introduction of a competitive examination for the BA at the beginning of the nineteenth century revealed that college lectures and classes on their own were insufficient to guarantee a high ranking. The ambitious therefore hired private coaches to improve their charges. John Henry Newman, a scholar of Trinity, took his BA in 1820: in the term before, he saw his coach for at least two hours a day and sometimes five.[35] Such exaggerated emphasis on examination success had a detrimental effect on the students' overall education. In the seventeenth and eighteenth centuries many undergraduates, with their tutors' blessing, found time to follow private courses in extracurricular subjects such as modern languages, dance and military drill. The foundation of the new chairs in the arts and sciences after 1750 offered students the opportunity to develop their knowledge at no cost in a number of fields not covered by the BA curriculum. At the beginning of the nineteenth century they responded positively. From 1820, however, they abandoned the professorial lectures in order to cram for 'honours'.[36]

INTELLECTUAL TORPOR

The medieval universities had been at the heart of Europe's intellectual life. Even if most, like Oxford, sheltered innovative

Gateway and cupola, front quadrangle, The Queen's College, 1733–36: Oxford's most gracious eighteenth-century quadrangle, chiefly the work of George Clarke (1661–1736), university benefactor.

minds only for a limited period, virtually all made a mark. The Reformation itself was born at the humble University of Wittenberg, which had not been founded until 1502. After Luther tore Christendom apart and Europe divided into confessional blocs, universities everywhere were more closely policed to ensure their teaching supported the local orthodoxy, and they lost their critical bite. Over the next 300 years the number of universities doubled – from 90 to 180 – but virtually every significant development in philosophy and science was the work of individuals beyond their walls. The universities made little contribution to the replacement of Aristotelian natural philosophy by a physics based on experiment and mathematics. Nor did they play an active part in the creation of a new science of man as an autonomous individual with natural rights, which culminated in the eighteenth century in the Enlightenment critique of church, state and society. Only the major advances in medicine during this period were largely the work of university professors. Isaac Newton's long and productive sojourn at Trinity College, Cambridge, was an anomaly.[37]

Oxford, a quintessential confessional university, was no different from elsewhere. It did not turn its back on new developments. Under the Laudian Code, it was supposed to uphold Aristotle and the ancients in perpetuity, but the best tutors from the mid seventeenth century introduced their pupils to new ideas as well as old. Most students in the eighteenth century followed a private course in the new experimental philosophy, and long before 1750 Aristotle had been effectively dethroned except in ethics. But for the most part Oxford was never a centre of creative thought. Many important scholars and scientists were educated at Oxford across the years, but few acquired their international standing while resident.

Both Thomas Hobbes (1588–1679) and Jeremy Bentham (1748–1832) were Oxford students, but no innovative philosopher resided at Oxford before the mid nineteenth century, apart from Locke, who was a fellow of Christ Church until expelled for his political views in 1684. Similarly, little important work was undertaken at the university for most of the period by adepts of the new physics. Oxford science chairs were often held by leading experimentalists but they did their productive work in and around London, where they had access to better facilities. Oxford was a centre of creative scientific thought only in the 1650s, when it housed a coterie of twenty to thirty experimental philosophers principally engaged in medical research inspired by William Harvey's discovery of the circulation of blood.[38] Most of the group were significant figures: they included the chemist Robert Boyle (1627–1691) and his assistant Robert Hooke (1635–1703), the young mathematician Christopher Wren (1632–1723) and the pioneer of the physiology of the brain Thomas Willis (1621–1675). But their presence in Oxford during the Interregnum reflected their hostility to the republican government and its church policies. With the Restoration, most departed for London in search of more lucrative patronage in the capital.

Oxford's furtherance of classical scholarship was hardly more inspiring. The university sheltered many competent Hellenists over the period, as its important contribution to the King James Bible of 1611 makes clear. An Oxford team led by Sir Henry Savile (1549–1622), warden of Merton, was largely responsible for translating the New Testament. Nonetheless, an ambitious attempt in the late seventeenth century, centred on Christ Church, to provide undergraduates with accessible editions of the Greek classics demonstrated that the quality was thinly spread. When a particularly sloppy edition of *Phalaris* was published in 1695, Oxford became an international laughing stock.[39] There was only one area of ancient-language study where the university gained a lasting and deserved European reputation: Hebrew and Arabic. In the second half of the seventeenth century especially, the university had few rivals in the field: Edward Pococke (1604–1691) and Thomas Smith (1638–1710) in particular stood head and shoulders above all but a handful of continental Hebraists, the first particularly famous for his work on the Mishnah.[40] Oxford, too, at the turn of the eighteenth century, led the way in the study of Old English and Anglo-Saxon antiquities through the efforts of scholars such as Edward Thwaites (1667–1711) of Queen's and Thomas Hearne (1678–1735) of St Edmund Hall. It was Hearne who oversaw the first published edition of *The Battle of Maldon*. But their insular research inevitably spawned little interest abroad.

As Oxford was effectively reduced to an undergraduate university after the Civil War, its cultural stock might have fallen further than that of most of its peers, where at least the higher studies of theology, law and medicine continued to flourish. It was certainly heavily criticized at home in the first part of the nineteenth century by writers in the *Edinburgh Review* who believed that the university should be open to non-Anglicans and that much greater emphasis should be placed in the BA curriculum on mathematics and science.[41] One of their number, the erstwhile Oxford student Sir William Hamilton, even took issue with the tutors, claiming that, as a group, they contained 'an infinitely smaller proportion of men of literary reputation, than among the actual instructors of any other University in the world'. They were incompetent, ignorant and an impediment to learning.[42] In the wider world, however, Oxford, for all its curricular deficiencies, always had a mystique. Hardly any foreigner came to study – it was even more of a national university than in the Late Middle Ages – but many from all walks of life came to visit.

John Wesley (1703–1791), tutor and fellow of Lincoln College and father of Methodism. Portrait by Nathaniel Hone, c.1766.

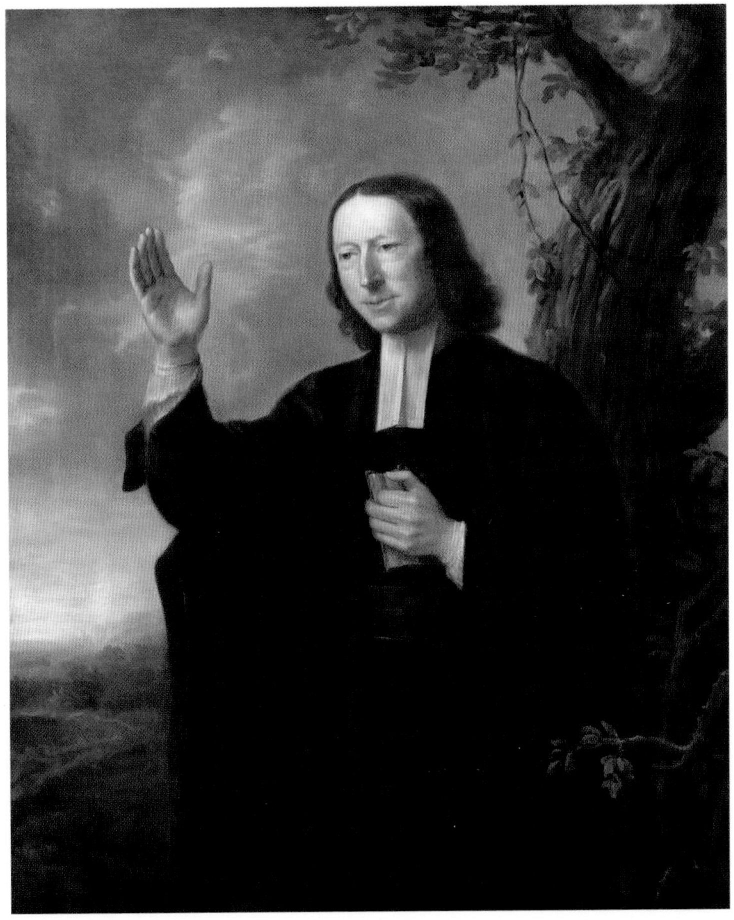

What drew scholars were Oxford's libraries, in particular the Bodleian, the refurbished and extended library built by the university in the late fifteenth century to house the collection of Humfrey, duke of Gloucester. Reopened in 1602 and rechristened after its new benefactor, Sir Thomas Bodley (1545–1613), the university's library quickly expanded its holdings. In 1700 a former member of the university, Edward Chamberlayn (1616–1703), judged it the equal, if not the superior, of its

The Radcliffe Camera from the east: opened in 1749, it was built with a benefaction from the Oxford physician John Radcliffe (1650–1714), here depicted surrounded by three figures representing medicine, benevolence and fame. From the *Oxford Almanac* (1752).

foreign competitors.[43] In 1850 it contained 250,000 books and a vast number of priceless manuscripts that scholars from all over Europe wanted to consult. The less academically minded came to explore the buildings. In the 1530s the university had virtually none of its own. By 1750, thanks to the generosity of a succession of donors, it had constructed a cluster of architecturally interesting buildings in the vicinity of the Divinity School, which gave it a powerful visual presence: the Schools Quadrangle (1603–14), the new Convocation House (1640), the Sheldonian Theatre (1669), the Old Ashmolean

(1667–83), the Clarendon Building (1710–13) and the Radcliffe Camera (1749). The colleges, too, continually extended and improved their sites across the period, as we have seen. As a result, no other university in Europe, except Cambridge, possessed such an array of beautiful buildings in different styles. For visitors to England on the northern grand tour, the University of Oxford was on their list of places they had to see.

Oxford's international reputation was also sustained by its university press, which gave its handful of serious scholars an opportunity to get their work into print and to gain an audience abroad.[44] Put on a firm footing in the late seventeenth century through the efforts of the dean of Christ Church, John Fell (1625–1686), the press was described by a foreign visitor as early as 1710 as 'far famed'.[45] In the first half of the nineteenth century, under the management of the regius professor of Greek, Thomas Gaisford (1779–1855), it spread its wings and began to publish works by German scholars as well. The press gave the university an edge over Cambridge. After the Reformation the Fenland university had developed in much the same way as Oxford, and from the mid seventeenth century it was also reduced to an undergraduate school dominated by the heads of the colleges. It largely escaped censure after 1800 because its BA curriculum placed a greater emphasis on mathematics. But it too lacked scholars of substance after Newton's departure and relied on its majestic libraries and buildings to keep it in the limelight. Unlike Oxford, however, this was all there was: Cambridge had no vibrant press to mask its intellectual weakness.

Oxford in the Age of Empire

REFORM AND RECONSTRUCTION

At the turn of the nineteenth century Britain was already in the throes of industrialization but it was still a largely aristocratic and confessional state and society. Beginning in the late 1820s, the country was gradually transformed over the next hundred years into a modern secular and democratic society that paid lip service at least to the idea of fostering the talents of all. At the same time, it acquired the largest empire the world had ever known. In the first half of the nineteenth century Oxford was a confessional university that offered a narrow curriculum and principally served the Church of England and the squirearchy. By 1850 it looked increasingly out of date in the new industrial and imperial Britain where the university marketplace was also becoming more crowded. Scotland had long had five universities of its own which had active higher faculties and were socially more open. Edinburgh in particular was renowned for its medical teaching. But by 1850 there were rivals in England as well with the foundation of the non-sectarian University of London in 1836 and three new Anglican colleges in Wales, the north and the capital. And the foundations continued. On the eve of the Second World War, there were universities all over the empire and eleven, including Oxford and Cambridge, in England itself.[46] In this new world of the competitive university, had Oxford not addressed its deficiencies, it might well have disappeared from the academic map.

The easiest shortcoming to address was the curriculum, which was done by multiplying the number of arts courses or 'schools' that an Oxford student might take.[47] In 1850 Convocation divided the existing BA examination into four schools: Literae Humaniores, or Lit. Hum. (classical language, literature and philosophy); Mathematics; Natural Science; and Modern History and Jurisprudence, which became separate

'College Comforts: A Freshman Taking Possession of his Rooms': cartoon exaggerating the poor condition in which some students left their college accommodation on going down. Drawn and engraved by George Cruikshank, 1824.

subjects from 1873. By 1940 a further six schools had been added: Theology (1869); Oriental Languages (1886); English Language and Literature (1893); Modern Languages (1903); Philosophy, Politics and Economics (1920); and Geography (1930). Natural Science always remained a single school but from the 1870s undergraduates were allowed to specialize in one of a growing number of sciences, including engineering from 1909. Initially, to gain a BA candidates had to take Lit. Hum. and one other subject, but gradually the emphasis on classics was relaxed. From 1886 Oxford students could avoid taking a course in classics completely, though they always had to show a proficiency in Latin before they could be admitted to the university.[48] Gradually, too, students studying a particular

The Exeter College Eight on the Isis: an early depiction of an intercollegiate rowing race passing Christ Church Meadow. Watercolour by William Turner, 1824.

discipline had to read for an honours degree. Weaker students could still read for a pass, but by the end of the nineteenth century they were members of a separate school which had its own general curriculum.[49] Until 1872 the schools had no institutional identity but were looked after by ad hoc committees appointed annually by the proctors. In that year they were entrusted to elected boards of studies which drew up the curriculum and set the examinations, while the teaching

remained the responsibility of the college tutors. Until 1882 the boards were all part of a nominal faculty of arts. Thereafter, they slowly metamorphosed into separate faculties, whose activities from 1912 were overseen by the General Board, a committee of representatives of the different subjects chaired by the vice-chancellor. At the turn of the twentieth century, therefore, and for the first time in its history, Oxford had a faculty organization, but it no longer had a faculty of arts.

Bringing an end to the *ancien régime* university proved more difficult but was slowly achieved. From the 1830s there was a body of support within the university for wholesale reform, especially among the professors and some of the younger tutors, but the college heads dug in their heels. Ultimately reform was forced upon Oxford by Parliament. A Royal Commission was appointed to look into Oxford's governance, which reported in May 1852. It made two chief demands. First, the Hebdomadal Board must be made more representative of the wider body of fellows and professors; and, second, college fellowships and scholarships must be opened up to all and be awarded on merit after an examination, as was already the case at Oriel and Balliol. The university demurred, but Parliament, at the urging of Gladstone, one of the university's two MPs, responded by passing an act on 7 May 1854 which knocked the heads of house off their pedestal, made Congregation rather than Convocation the principal deliberative and electoral body, and ended the Anglican monopoly – henceforth students of any confession or none could attend Oxford. The act also set up a new commission to reform the colleges' statutes, which largely brought to an end the role of patronage in elections to scholarships and fellowships and made them much more competitive.

Further parliamentary assaults on the old Oxford followed. Under the 1854 legislation, college fellows still had to be Anglicans. In 1871 a further Act of Parliament, piloted by

Gladstone, ended this requirement too. Then the colleges' wealth came under scrutiny. A Royal Commission which reported in 1874 laid bare for the first time the huge income of the richer colleges compared with the university's. This gave birth to a second Commission in 1877, which ordered an annual transfer of wealth between the two in order to increase the number of professors and readers, updated the university's statutes in 1882 and oversaw a fresh revision of the colleges' statutes to ensure their endowments were used wisely. Too many fellows, it was revealed, even if now appointed on merit, were treating their position as a sinecure rather than engaging in postgraduate study. Henceforth, fellows who were not tutors had to demit after seven years, or at least face periodic re-election, when their scholarly achievements would be scrutinized. Other aspects of the old clerical Oxford were also slowly set aside from the mid nineteenth century. The requirement that most fellows be in orders largely disappeared from the 1850s, and the demand that they live in and be celibate twenty years later. The colleges remained Anglican enclaves in that their chapels survived the reforms intact and their daily Anglican service remained a central part of college life, but to all intents and purposes Oxford in 1900 had become a secular institution.

By then the university had also ceased to be a male preserve. All over the western world in the second half of the nineteenth century, there were calls that women be admitted to higher education. Oxford responded slightly more slowly than Cambridge to the demand but there was little opposition to the request provided women and men lived apart, and in 1879 it permitted the establishment of two female hostels or halls: Lady Margaret Hall and Somerville, the one High Church, the other Low. Two further halls were founded in 1886 and 1893 – St Hugh's and St Hilda's – and the number of female students slowly rose. Women never formed more than a small

John Henry Newman (1801–1890), fellow and tutor of Oriel, leading light of the Oxford Movement, Roman Catholic convert and author of *The Idea of a University* (1873). Portrait by Sir John Everett Millais, 1881.

THE BREAKFAST PARTY.
Collegian —— "So Mr Slowcoach wishes to see me for having cut his Lecture does he? Then give him my most affectionate regards and say I am confined to my Rooms with a severe attack of aggravated Consumption!

'The Breakfast Party': a satirical comment on the indolent student's casual approach to his studies. From *College Life: A Series of Original Etchings by Edward Bradley* (1849–50).

proportion of the intake, however, and in 1927 their numbers were capped at 840. They were also subject to much closer supervision than their male counterparts and, before the First World War, could go out only in pairs or suitably chaperoned. Even taking a degree was denied them until 1920, although they were permitted to sit the examinations. All the same, women gradually escaped from the margins of the university and by the 1930s were an accepted presence.

Seriously broadening the university's social intake, on the other hand, proved virtually impossible, though it was a continual bone of contention. The issue was particularly raised immediately after the First World War by yet another Royal Commission on Oxford, this time chaired by the former prime minister Herbert Asquith (1852–1928). Critics of the status quo were adamant that the principal problem was cost. Residence at Oxford was expensive. Even in the mid nineteenth century, according to the 1850 Commission's report, a student needed £150 per annum just to live frugally. If the expense could be reduced, then the social intake could be widened.[50] No attempt was made to solve the problem by resurrecting the medieval halls as a cheaper alternative. Indeed, the only one that still survived by 1914 was St Edmund Hall, which had had a continuous existence for 600 years. There were several new halls founded at the turn of the twentieth century but these were for members of the Roman Catholic regular orders and for Protestant dissenters and evangelicals who wanted to live a communal existence apart.[51] Instead, two other routes for broadening access were touted and tried. The first was to permit undergraduates to reside at Oxford in lodgings without belonging to a college or hall. This was possible from 1868–9 and by the 1890s there were regularly some 200 non-collegiates at Oxford in any one year, divided into two separate societies for men and women, a larger group than all but one or two colleges could muster. The second was to found a new college where costs would be deliberately kept low. Initial attempts in the 1860s foundered but finally bore fruit with the establishment of Keble in 1870 and a revivified Hertford College four years later. Keble was named after a leading Tractarian, John Keble (1792–1866), who had stayed loyal to the university and the Church of England. Built in neo-Gothic red brick, not dressed stone, from a subscription raised among the High Church phalanx, it offered no-frills accommodation for those who wanted to live in an old-fashioned confessional environment.

By 1911 it too had 200 students. According to the chancellor, Viscount Curzon (1859–1925), in 1909, non-collegiates could cover their annual basic costs for as little as £52, Keble students for £85.[52]

Neither development seems to have greatly extended the university's social profile. Oxford did have some success in that it ceased to be a university that simply recruited from landed or clerical families. By 1897–8 as many as 64 per cent of the male intake had fathers in business or the old and new professions. But attracting many students from lower down the social scale proved a forlorn hope. In 1897–8 only 5 per cent of male matriculands hailed from the lower middle or working class; the figure was still only 10 per cent forty years later, despite all the efforts to improve the situation. Even the non-collegiates came from a privileged background. The problem still remained one of cost. There were no state or local government grants for poor students before 1902, and they had difficulty competing successfully for the colleges' 400 scholarships when they had only been to a local grammar and not a pukka public school.[53] The future Master of the Rolls, Alfred 'Tom' Denning (1899–1999), entered Magdalen in 1916 to read mathematics. His father was a Whitchurch draper. He had a college exhibition worth £30 and a Hampshire county scholarship worth £50. This was not enough in a college notoriously full of Old Etonians and he had to skimp on his accommodation and heating. 'Father could not help. But I determined to accept it – and manage the best I could. Go without if need be.'[54]

Oxford's numbers steadily grew over the period. There were 2,000 undergraduates in residence in 1860 and 4,391 in 1938–9. Yet its failure to broaden its social profile meant it was always an elitist university compared to its rivals in the provinces and the capital, which mainly drew on a local clientele who lived at home.[55] So too was Cambridge, which had looked nearly as

Benjamin Jowett (1817–1893), tutor and master of Balliol, vice-chancellor and enthusiastic believer in the intellectual and moral benefits of an Oxford education. Watercolour by Julia Janet Georgiana [Duncan], Lady Abercromby, 1892.

University Museum of Natural History, opened in 1860: purpose-built as a space for teaching and research in the natural sciences. Its huge glass roof supported on an iron frame is a wonder of Victorian architecture.

antediluvian in 1850 and had undergone similar parliamentary scrutiny and internal reform to drag it into the modern world. Nonetheless, this did not mean that by 1939 Oxford and Cambridge enjoyed a negligible share of the United Kingdom's university population. As 85 per cent of children never had a secondary education before the Second World War, the pool of potential recruits was small. Nor was there much call for a higher education among the minority who had had extended schooling. From the mid nineteenth century the number of professions in the new industrial society was growing fast. But, in contrast to the Continent, most professional men and women trained on the job, even solicitors. In consequence the new universities, whatever their dreams, had no more success than the old in persuading large numbers of young men and women to take their degree courses: most of their graduates went into school teaching. There were only 50,000 full-time university students in the United Kingdom in 1939. Oxford and Cambridge between them still accounted for 20 per cent of the total, and they remained the largest universities. Rich parents who sought a university education for their offspring were never tempted to send them elsewhere. Oxford and Cambridge were always much more attractive than the new foundations on account of the perceived superiority of their undergraduate education.

Keble College Chapel, opened in 1870: the focal point of the new brick-built college dedicated to High Anglicanism and frugal living.

THE OXFORD EXPERIENCE

An Oxford undergraduate education became world famous from the end of the nineteenth century because it claimed to do more than impart knowledge. The *Edinburgh Review* had attacked unreformed Oxford for privileging classical literature and philosophy above science and mathematics. Undergraduate studies should be useful and the Oxford curriculum was too narrow. Edward Copleston (1776–1849), provost of Oriel, fought

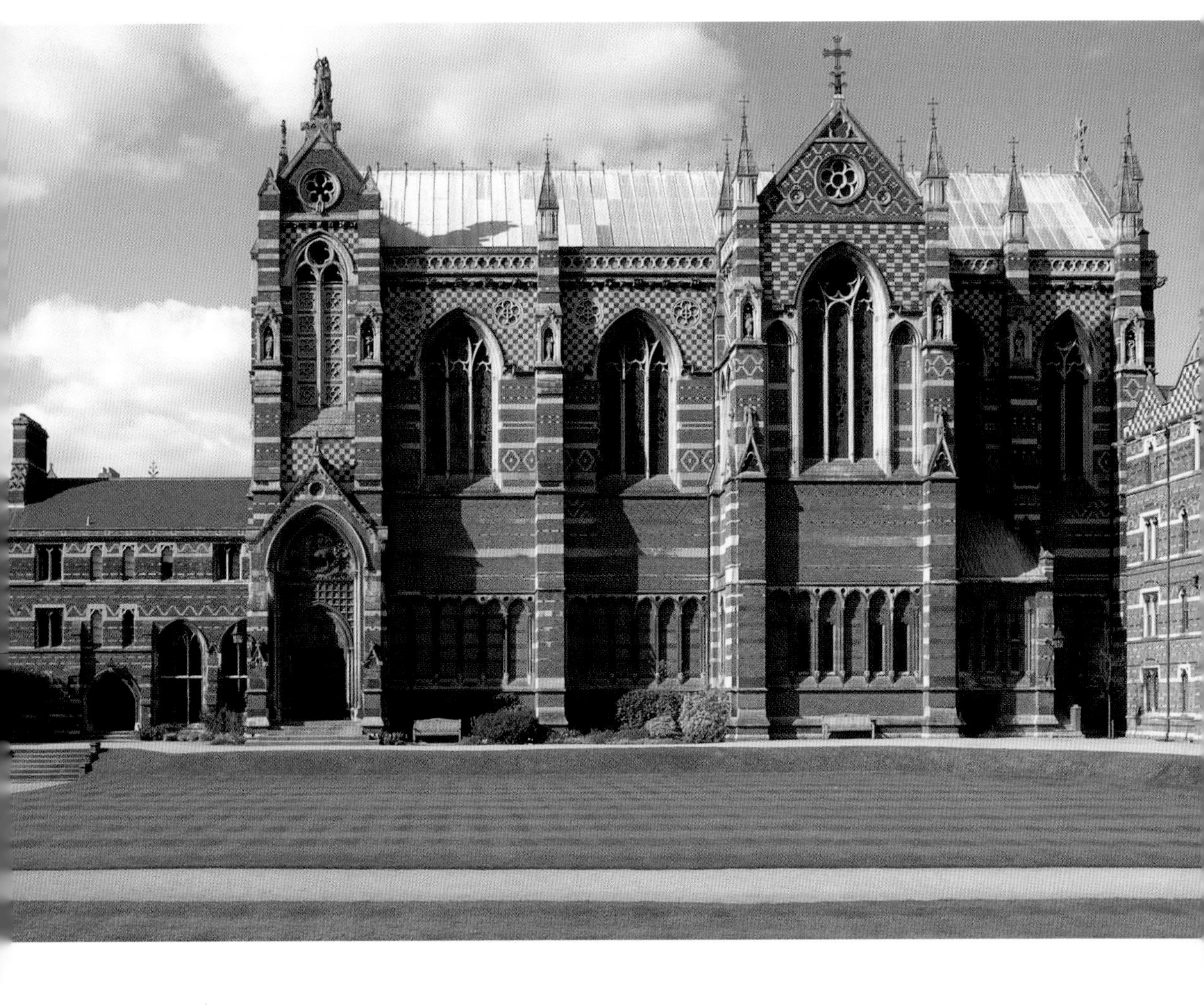

Lady Margaret Hall, Deneke Common Room, 1933: an example of the relatively quiet, domestic and segregated life of most Oxford female students before the Second World War.

back for the university by claiming that its uselessness was a virtue. Oxford deliberately eschewed filling the heads of the young with practical information. It aimed rather, through studying the ancients, to build character by training the mind, discouraging idle speculation and creating solid citizens who could turn their hand to any business of life.[56] Copleston's argument, a refinement of the Renaissance humanists' justification for studying the culture of the classical world, became a mantra repeated down the generations and adapted to fit a reformed university in which Lit. Hum. was just one of a number of undergraduate schools. Its most sophisticated exponent was John Henry Newman, who, after he had left Oxford and gone over to Rome, delivered a series of lectures in Dublin in 1852 on the subject.[57] But before 1914 the mantra was reprised endlessly in a more simplistic form in chapel sermons and the pep talks of college heads. An Oxford education was supposed to be transformative. Out of the university's womb would emerge a benign race of Christian supermen who would dedicate their lives to doing good and serving the empire in different ways. Scientists as well as artists were agreed that nothing should be taught at Oxford that would have an immediate or obvious practical value. Engineering became acceptable as a degree course only once it was agreed that the undergraduates would not receive any workshop training. The bloodbath of the First World War greatly reduced the university's enthusiasm for the empire and Christian gentility. But the belief that an Oxford undergraduate education was peculiarly valuable because it trained the mind was not diminished. If anything, in the interwar years it was emphasized even more strongly.

The new universities taught their students through lectures where they passively absorbed information. Oxford never eschewed lectures but entrusted the task of honing the undergraduate mind to the personal college tutor, whose role became much more onerous. After 1850, rather than simply offering students moral and academic guidance, the tutor was entrusted with sharpening their wits through setting regular pieces of work and submitting their efforts to forensic scrutiny in face-to-face discussion. Students might officially joust with their tutor only once or twice a week in the 'tutorial hour'. But the best tutors were available day and night to discuss and comment on work in progress. The prototype was Benjamin Jowett (1817–1893), who was a Balliol tutor for thirty years in the mid nineteenth century before becoming the college's master. 'His greatest skill', according to George Brodrick (1831–1903), a future warden of Merton, 'consisted, like that of Socrates, in helping us to learn and think for ourselves ... No other tutor, within my experience, has ever approached him in the depth and extent of his pastoral supervision.'[58] And Jowett continued to shape the minds of his charges once term was over by taking them on study trips during the vacations.

With the establishment of a series of undergraduate schools, tutoring gradually became more professional. By the end of the nineteenth century, tutors were paid on a sliding scale according to age and experience, and had a retirement age and a pension; their appointment and organization were controlled in each college by a tutorial board chaired by an official called the senior tutor. Initially most tutors were classicists but it was soon recognized that specialists were needed to look after each school, and their number in each college grew. Ideally students were taught as much as possible in their own college from the belief that the relationship between tutor and pupil took time to develop and thrived on their close proximity. But the system, as it developed, was flexible. If the number of undergraduates in the college reading for a particular school was too few or the college too poor to support a post, then students were sent out to be looked after by an outside tutor. Most students too

Sir Thomas Herbert Warren (1853–1930), long-serving president of Magdalen, vice-chancellor and promoter of the virtues of team games. Spy cartoon by Sir Leslie Ward, *Vanity Fair*, 8 April 1893.

VANITY FAIR. April 8, 1893.

"Magdalen College, Oxford."

Thomas Herbert Warren

Students of Cherwell Hall, St Hilda's College, 1900–1910: the female undergraduate was perceived as serious, sober and statuesque.

would be tutored externally on the occasional paper. Even the best-informed tutors could not cover the whole curriculum, so tutors in different colleges exchanged pupils according to their expertise. Colleges became unhappy with the arrangement only when recourse to out-college tutors became too frequent. Magdalen's science tutor Robert Gunther (1869–1940) was forced to resign after the First World War because his subject was zoology, which few students read, and he could no longer even teach the first-year chemistry course which had hitherto justified his retention.

Not every tutor lived up to Jowett's billing. Many were guilty of cramming their students for the examinations rather than stimulating thought. But the best subjected their tutees to an exhausting and remorseless grilling which taught them to express themselves precisely and clearly. Harold Joachim (1868–1938), a 'Greats', or classics, tutor at Merton in the early twentieth century, was merciless. A student who passed through his hands in 1914, the philosopher G.R.G. Mure (1893–1979), concluded that 'for a long time I got little from the discussion of my weekly essay but a most humbling conviction of my own futility'. Joachim would pull his work to pieces. 'What I found quite shattering was Joachim's habit of taking a sentence or two from one's essay and assuming with a more than Socratic courtesy that one must have meant something definite when one wrote them. It soon became evident that one had not.'[59] Some students wilted under the treatment. A young woman of St Hugh's in the early twentieth century, after a tutorial with the historian of political thought A.J. Carlyle (1861–1943), admitted to her diary to feeling 'in a somewhat headless condition hav[ing] had this part of the anatomy bitten off'.[60] But most victims survived intact and in later life realized the benefits of being put through the mill.

While the tutors taught the students to think, collegiate life was supposed to develop their character. Richer students belonged to private dining societies, often drank too much and caused mayhem, at least within the college. In 1894 after one bibulous dinner, all the windows in Christ Church's Peckwater Quad were broken. But rowdyism was a reaction to the strict code of self-control that the university sought to impose. Like the top public schools from which so many male students came, Oxford before the First World War aimed to instil Christian manliness, an amalgam of diligence, loyalty, respect for others and self-sacrifice, which had been initially promoted at Rugby by Thomas Arnold (1795–1842), briefly Oxford professor of modern history.[61] This was an ethic crudely hammered home in the homilies of the heads of house. Sir Herbert Warren (1853–1930), president of Magdalen, reminded his undergraduates in 1885 that they lived in a palace and must prove worthy tenants, embracing a common Christian purpose. There was no room for cliques or 'the baleful creations of vice and selfishness and sensuality'.[62] But the code was principally learnt on the river or the college playing field. There had been no college or university team sports before 1850 apart from rowing – the first Oxford and Cambridge boat race took place in 1829. In the second half of the nineteenth century, the college authorities became convinced that sport inculcated *esprit de corps*, endurance and a sense of fair play, and its cultivation was encouraged. By the late nineteenth century virtually every male undergraduate spent his afternoons rowing or playing games. Intercollegiate sporting contests were great occasions when the whole college turned out to cheer.

From the 1880s the tutorial system and competitive sport drew students to Oxford from all over the world. The influx was greatly stimulated by the establishment of the Rhodes Scholarship scheme in 1902, which within four years was supporting 161 students from the empire, the United States and Germany. To what extent students from home or abroad left Oxford with a sharper edge to their minds and their characters suitably embellished is anyone's guess. Some definitely burnt with a desire to help mankind. On going down, they worked initially as volunteers in various missions to the poorer parts of London set up by individual colleges at the end of the nineteenth century. Others, also presumably anxious to spread enlightenment, entered the British or a branch of the Imperial Civil Service. But a declining minority now took orders and most Oxford graduates ended up in the private professions.

Student dining club, Corpus Christi College, c.1900: the hedonism of the affluent male undergraduate.

What is clear is that many of the Edwardian generation never lived to have the chance to make a difference, for 15,000 Oxford men served in the First World War and 3,000 paid the ultimate sacrifice. The heroes were legion, and many won the Victoria Cross. The former Trinity student and medical officer Noel Godfrey Chavasse (1884–1917) was the only member of Britain's armed forces during the conflict to be awarded the highest honour twice.

Oxford University and the First World War: the university's Examination Schools on the High Street, opened in 1883, became part of the army's 3rd Southern General Hospital.

While the slaughter of the First World War seriously eroded support for Christian manliness, it did nothing to dampen the enthusiasm for team games. At the same time, the more intense emphasis in the 1920s and 1930s on teaching students to think and express themselves clearly did encourage the foundation of college clubs devoted to non-sporting activities. By 1900 the university possessed a highly valued and longstanding debating society, the Oxford Union, founded in 1823, and numerous political, musical and theatrical clubs to which undergraduates could belong. However, the colleges were not well supplied with clubs of their own. Virtually every college by 1890 had a Junior Common Room, which provided students with newspapers and other basic services. But other college clubs tended to be disreputable dining societies. Between the wars, in contrast, college clubs devoted to the performance arts, especially drama, proliferated. According to the future general secretary of the Trades Union Congress, George Woodcock (1904–1979), there were twelve non-sporting societies at New College in the early 1930s. These included the XX Club, whose members gave witty speeches 'almost invariably delivered in an attempted imitation of the style of some famous past or present parliamentary or after-dinner speaker'.[63]

Among Britain's other universities, only Cambridge, which embraced a similar anti-utilitarian rationale and shared a similar clientele, could offer such extracurricular riches.

DOMINUS
MEA

The rest sought to provide sporting and social facilities, but they lacked the ethos and the funds needed to make them a substantial part of university life. Moreover, as they were largely non-residential universities, student interest was limited.

TOWARDS A RESEARCH CULTURE

As a training ground for undergraduates, Oxford was accepted as one of the two top universities in Britain and the empire in 1939. But in the first half of the twentieth century universities were no longer simply judged on the quality of their teaching but also on their contribution to research. The advancement of learning had never been part of Oxford's remit before 1800. Although lecturers and professors in their courses might lead students down interesting and original avenues, this was never part of the job description. As we saw earlier, the Scientific Revolution largely occurred outside the universities. In the eighteenth century, pioneering work in the arts and sciences was promoted by a new institution, the learned academy, which was a forum for both the discussion and the publication of research. At the beginning of the nineteenth century, however, the Prussian philosopher Wilhelm von Humboldt (1767–1835) developed a new concept of the university where professors would be involved in the furtherance of knowledge as well as its dissemination, which he argued would be to the benefit of both. This new ideal was embodied from the beginning at the new University of Berlin founded in 1810 by the Prussian king. Thereafter, it was slowly taken up in other German universities before spreading to the rest of Europe and the United States in the last quarter of the nineteenth century.

Before 1914 Oxford paid little more than lip service to the Humboldtian ideal. The mid-nineteenth-century reformers had wanted to reform the undergraduate university: they had no interest in making Oxford a centre of original research. As late as 1868, one of their number, Mark Pattison (1813–1884), rector of Lincoln, insisted that the professors' duty was 'to maintain, cultivate and diffuse extant knowledge'. This was a commonplace function and not to be confused with 'the very exceptional pursuit of prosecuting researches or conducting experiments with a view to new discoveries'.[64] The British state, conversely, convinced that the rise of Germany as an economic power after unification was due to the research vitality of its universities, had been taken with the ideal since the 1870s. In consequence, under Oxford's new statutes of 1882, professors and readers, if not college tutors, were expected to engage in research as well as teach. But the new dispensation had limited immediate effect. The university certainly had a number of active researchers in its midst in the late Victorian and Edwardian eras. Figures such as the Sanskrit expert Friedrich Max Müller (1823–1900), the archaeologist Arthur Evans (1851–1941) and the crystallographer H.A. Miers (1858–1942) had international reputations. On the eve of the First World War, too, a number of young researchers working in Oxford were about to make their mark, such as the chemist 'Harry' Moseley (1887–1915), who had found a new way to bring rigour to the periodic table. Such figures, however, were exceptional.

The university had done little, moreover, to develop the next generation of scholars and scientists by promoting postgraduate studies. It had good library resources, obviously, and reasonable if limited laboratory space in the growing assortment of buildings around the University Museum, opened for science teaching in 1860. But Oxford offered next to no formal research training. It was possible from the 1890s to take a postgraduate diploma in a number of subjects which were not at that date part of the undergraduate curriculum, such as geography, economics and anthropology. It was possible, too, to submit original work to the university and be awarded a DLitt or a DSc. But in 1914 Oxford had still not instituted a research doctorate. The only substantial higher degree that Oxford possessed at that date was in medicine, the one faculty of the unreformed university that had not been subsumed in the undergraduate course. Students who wanted to take the degree – and the number increased after 1870 – had first to take a BA in the physiology specialism of the Natural Science School. They then studied theoretical medicine at Oxford and the clinical component of the degree elsewhere, because there were limited facilities before the Second World War for hands-on learning in the relatively small city hospital.

The situation began to improve only with the outbreak of the First World War. In 1909, shortly after becoming the university's chancellor, George Curzon lambasted the university for its lack of interest in research. Oxford had to come to terms with the fact that it was 'now an accepted axiom that it is a portion of the duty of the oldest Universities to train their members for the exploration of remote as well as the survey of well-trodden fields'.[65] Over the following years he and his supporters strove to place research at the heart of the university. The DPhil was introduced in 1917 and a number of Britain's most creative scientists were lured to professorial posts, including the neurologist Sir Charles Sherrington (1857–1952), the chemist Frederick Soddy (1877–1956) and the physicist Frederick Lindemann (1886–1957). Soddy quickly repaid the investment by becoming the first Oxford professor in post to win a Nobel Prize. Curzon's efforts were seconded by the Asquith Commission's report in 1922. This called on tutors as well as professors to engage in research and was particularly anxious that Oxford invested more heavily in the sciences, which were seen as the key to success if there was ever a second global conflict. Oxford responded positively on both counts.

Nuffield College: founded in 1937 with a benefaction from the motor magnate William Richard Morris, Lord Nuffield (1877–1963), Nuffield's buildings were not complete until 1962. It was Oxford's first college for postgraduate students.

A new generation of tutors accepted that research was part of their remit and began to take sabbaticals in other universities abroad. Leslie Sutton, elected a chemistry tutor at Magdalen in 1935, believed his colleagues should be made to see the world and, if need be, 'escorted to the boat'.[66] At the same time, the university worked hard to improve its facilities. It actively raised funds to establish new professorships and put up new buildings, especially in the vicinity of the University Museum to the north of South Parks Road, which became known as the Science Area. When war broke out in 1939, it had just opened a new physics laboratory, its first purpose-built inorganic chemistry laboratory was on the drawing board and a large extension to the Bodleian Library was all but complete.[67] In Viscount Nuffield (1877–1963), the father of the Oxford motor industry, the university found a particularly munificent donor. In the course of the 1930s he helped set up St Peter's, the one new undergraduate college of the interwar years, and gave £2 million to establish a research school in clinical medicine and a further £1 million to set up a postgraduate college in accountancy and engineering.

Oxford's research profile was boosted in the 1930s with the arrival of exiles from Nazi and Fascist tyranny. The study of the classical world, always an Oxford strong point, was further strengthened by the appointment of Eduard Fraenkel (1888–1970), late of Freiburg, to the chair of Latin in 1934, while the eventual election of the Austrian musicologist Egon Wellesz (1885–1974) to a fellowship at Lincoln would lead to the foundation of the Faculty of Music in 1944. But it was the physical sciences that benefited most from the influx of Jewish and Christian scholars and scientists. The most famous German import, Albert Einstein (1879–1955), who had been made a fellow of Christ Church in 1931, stayed only a couple of years, but he was replaced by another big fish, the quantum theorist

Erwin Schrödinger (1887–1961), who was awarded a Nobel Prize within a few weeks of his arrival. Even more importantly, Lindemann single-handedly recruited central Europe's leading experimentalists in the fields of superconductivity and superfluidity, thereby turning Oxford overnight into the world centre for low-temperature physics. The immigrants were relatively few in number but they were a breath of fresh air. Although students from the Dominions and the United States had been attending Oxford since the late nineteenth century and some had been given posts, the university was still dominated in the 1930s by British-born and public-school-educated Protestants. The exiles laid the foundations of its cosmopolitan future.

However, Oxford's significance as a centre of research on the eve of the Second World War should not be exaggerated. In the sciences, if not the arts, Cambridge, which had been making an important contribution to the advancement of physics from the 1870s, remained far ahead of its rival. A number of the British provincial universities, too, had important research schools, in particular Manchester, which had played a seminal role in the development of the study of history. Most of Oxford's scientific stars in the interwar years had made their reputations elsewhere. Soddy had been poached from Aberdeen and Sherrington from Liverpool. For all the vibrancy of the research teams headed by the leading professors, there were still few postgraduates of any kind at the university. In 1938–9 there were 536, just over 12 per cent of the undergraduate total. Even Oxford's commitment to the physical sciences was not absolute. Nuffield's wishes for a new postgraduate college were ignored. The university duly used the benefactor's money to establish Nuffield College but it was dedicated to promoting postgraduate study in the social sciences.

The World University

THE NEW HIGHER-EDUCATIONAL ORDER

In Oxford's case the Second World War was less murderous than the First – 1,719 Oxonians, men and women, lost their lives in the conflict. But, unlike its predecessor, the war proved a turning point in Oxford's history. The university which emerged in the years after 1945 was different in scale, purpose and structure.

In the second half of the twentieth century, states all over the world placed a novel emphasis on the value of higher education. The idea that had been around in Britain since the 1870s that universities could play a vital role in economic growth and defence was enthusiastically embraced by every government in the West and large amounts of taxpayers' money put aside to develop their research role, especially in the sciences. Governments also felt that a university education should no longer be the preserve of the rich but should be open to all who had the potential to benefit from it, both male and female. This belief became a state imperative with the emergence of the new digital economy from the 1980s, as it was believed that only countries with a well-educated population would be able to compete in the new global age. In consequence, more and more 18-year-olds were encouraged to enter higher education and the number of universities was rapidly expanded. From the turn of the millennium fast-developing countries like China and India followed suit. By 2012, in the world as whole there were 17,000 universities enrolling 153 million students. Britain was slower than most western states to develop a mass university system but by the year 2000 it had caught up with its neighbours and nearly 50 per cent of its 18-year-olds were in higher education. In 2016–17, Britain had 2.3 million full- and part-time students spread over 168 universities or equivalent institutions awarding degrees, while the British university system consumed £35 billion annually and employed 410,000 people in 2015–16.[68]

Perspective drawing of the New Bodleian Library, 1936. Although completed in 1940, the extension to the Bodleian by Sir Giles Gilbert Scott was officially opened only in 1946. It heralded the dawn of the postwar expansion of Oxford.

The New Bodleian Library: original design, signed by the architect, Sir Giles Gilbert Scott (1880–1960), and drawn by [illegible], passed by the University's Hebdomadal Council for release to the press, 1936. © Bodleian Library, Oxford

The huge worldwide expansion of higher education completely changed the context in which the University of Oxford existed. On the eve of the Second World War it had a small research arm but was principally a private teaching university that served the limited needs for higher education of Britain's public-school-educated male elite. Had it not adapted to the new circumstances, it could easily have become the British equivalent of an American liberal arts college. As it was, Oxford read the runes and largely embraced the new order with enthusiasm with the aim of maintaining its position as one of Britain's two leading universities. On the one hand, it tackled its elitist image as an undergraduate university for toffs. On the other, it threw itself into establishing a reputation as a research leviathan. From 1922 the university had received a government subsidy of £100,000 annually, which allowed it to increase its number of science teachers and researchers. After 1945 it had no qualms about accepting much greater government largesse to fund new posts, buildings and postgraduate students as well as particular research projects. By 1964–65 it relied on the state for 80 per cent of its income and had become a public university in all but name. When government generosity waned in the 1980s following the shock to the economy of the 1973 oil crisis, Oxford equally had few qualms about seeking money for further expansion from private donors. By 2015–16, thanks to a series of financial appeals, private donations and an annual subsidy from the profits of Oxford University Press, it had greatly improved its research base. By then its income of £1,322 million was fifty times higher in real terms than the figure in the 1930s, but only 50 per cent of it came from the state.[69]

These changes, too, were effected without undue pressure from outside. After the Asquith Commission of the early 1920s, Oxford was subject to no further parliamentary investigation into its governance. On two occasions, the university held its

St Catherine's College, 1962: built to a modern design by the Danish architect Arne Jacobsen (1901–1972), St Catherine's broke with tradition and had no quadrangle, gates or tower.

own internal inquiry. In 1964–66, a commission under the provost of Worcester, Lord Franks (1905–1993), looked at the university and its activities in its entirety; thirty years later another chaired by the vice-chancellor, Sir Peter North (b.1937), concentrated in particular on its governance. But both were set up at the university's prompting and allowed the university to bring its practices into line with political and social reality in its own way and consensually. In consequence, Oxford was able to adapt without destroying its most prominent traditional features. In 2015 Oxford remained a masters' or dons'[70] university where Congregation was the sovereign legislative body. It also remained a collegiate university, where every student, undergraduate or postgraduate had once more to belong to a college or a hall. As there were more college clubs and societies than ever before and intercollegiate sporting rivalry was just as intense, the college continued to be the centre of most students' social life. The colleges even competed against one another academically: from 1963 they were ranked annually according to their performance in Schools.

Student numbers increased fourfold between 1940 and 2015, so sustaining Oxford's collegiate ethos required determined effort. Part of the increase was managed through the foundation of new colleges. St Edmund Hall, the last medieval hall, and St Anne's, the former non-collegiate society for women, became colleges in 1952; St Catherine's, the former non-collegiate society for men, followed in their footsteps ten years later, and Mansfield, the former Congregationalist private hall, in 1995.[71] In addition, thanks to large benefactions, a further six colleges were founded specifically for postgraduates – St Antony's (1950), Linacre (1962), St Cross (1965), Wolfson (1965), Green (1979) and Templeton (1983)[72] – while in the mid 1990s Harris Manchester was set up for mature students and Kellogg College for students on part-time courses run by the Department for Continuing Education.[73] But the bulk of the increase was made possible only by the existing colleges taking in many more students, which in turn required further investment in new residential buildings, libraries and sporting facilities. That most of the colleges found little difficulty in raising much of the money for these improvements from old members was a testament to the enduring strength of college loyalties.

By creatively submitting to the zeitgeist, Oxford has by the first decades of the second millennium been transformed into one of the finest research universities in the world in both the arts and the sciences. At the same time, it has retained its reputation as a leading undergraduate school. In the various world rankings which began to appear from the late 1990s, it was usually placed among the top five alongside Cambridge, which had equally ploughed a successful but perhaps more predictable furrow, given its early advantage as a centre of scientific research.[74]

THE UNDERGRADUATE UNIVERSITY

The number of undergraduates at Oxford in December 2016 was more than two and a half times higher than it had been in 1939: 11,728 compared to 4,391.[75] The university was also recruiting from a broader constituency. Oxford had its greatest success in changing the gender balance. Only 16 per cent of the undergraduates were women at the time of the Franks Report, but by 1991–2 the figure had risen to just over 40 per cent and in 2007–8 it reached a high point of 47.3 per cent.[76] The dramatic shift was achieved by ending single-sex colleges, both male and female. There were calls to admit women to the men's colleges from the late 1960s, and in May 1972 Congregation

Wolfson College, North Oxford, 1974: one of a number of colleges built for postgraduate students after the Second World War and the most palatial, thanks to the munificence of the Ford and Wolfson foundations.

allowed Wadham, Hertford, Brasenose, Jesus and St Catherine's to go ahead from October 1974. Five years later most of the other male and female colleges followed suit, with only St Hilda's steadfastly holding out until 2008. Some of the first women in the old men's colleges were met with hostility and subjected to unwanted sexual attention. By and large, though, women were made welcome and within a few years the friction had ceased. It proved less easy to reduce the proportion of undergraduates that had been to public school. Things began well. From constituting two-thirds of the male undergraduates in 1938–9, the fraction was cut to under a half by 1965–6. It would have fallen further but for the abolition of most of the state grammar schools in favour of a comprehensive system of secondary education. For many years, pupils from state schools found it difficult to compete with their privately educated peers for places, and it was 1999 before the public-school intake again fell below 50 per cent. The change must have had some effect on the social profile of the undergraduate body but probably not as much as was hoped. According to the Franks Report in 1966, 13 per cent of the intake was working class. Fifty years later still only 15 per cent came from families with an income lower than the mean national wage.[77] There was little change too in the geographical background of the students, who were predominantly British. Oxford had hopes of expanding its foreign intake. In 2005 the university announced that it would 'implement a vigorous programme of international recruitment'.[78] Ten years later the number of foreign undergraduates had risen but only to 18 per cent of the total.[79]

Oxford's undergraduate population never expanded to the same degree as most of its British rivals and it grew only slowly after 1990 when numbers elsewhere exploded. However, the number of applicants more than doubled between 1985 and 2010, which allowed the university to tighten the conditions

Dorothy Hodgkin (1910–1994), Nobel laureate in chemistry (1964). Hodgkin was fellow and tutor at Somerville College, and is Britain's only female science Nobel prizewinner.

of entry and raise the intellectual calibre of its undergraduates, whatever their background. This was an important factor in maintaining Oxford's reputation as a leading undergraduate university at the beginning of the new millennium. So was the continued high quality of its teaching. The structure of undergraduate education had not greatly changed across the second half of the twentieth century. Some new honours courses were added to the existing curriculum – especially, from the late 1960s, in the form of joint courses – but the structure of the undergraduate degree was not otherwise changed and for the most part continued to be examined by traditional three-hour papers. No significant alteration occurred either in the way the curriculum was taught. A greater emphasis was placed on dovetailing lectures and tutorials so that they were mutually reinforcing, but the tutorial remained at the heart of the teaching experience. Attacked by some outsiders as a luxury, its importance was emphasized by the Franks Commission in 1966. 'We intend that reading and writing, rather than listening, should continue to be the salient characteristics of the Oxford system.'[80] Thereafter, the tutorial was never seriously challenged. It was made more professional at the beginning of the twenty-first century when faculties began to encourage closer cooperation between tutors covering the same papers, but its essence remained the same. Its continual importance reflected the equally tenacious Oxford belief that the purpose of an undergraduate education, whatever the subject, was to teach a student to think. In the main, too, students continued to be taught by senior academics. In many British universities by the end of the twentieth century, undergraduates were frequently being looked after by graduate students. But the North Commission in 1997 made it clear that this was not a road Oxford would take. 'It is partly on this principle that Oxford's reputation for excellent undergraduate teaching rests.'[81]

THE RESEARCH UNIVERSITY

In July 2016 Oxford employed 1,817 academics in permanent, full-time posts. All were involved to different degrees in teaching and research. This was three and a half times the number in 1938–9.[82] Most of the increase came from the creation of university posts in new subjects, especially in the sciences, but there was an initial boost immediately after the Second World War when it was decided that in future college tutors should also hold a university lectureship and be contractually required to do research. Overnight a solid foundation was laid for the creation of the modern research university. Although it took several decades before every don on the payroll was actively engaged in productive research, the new research ethos was soon embedded in all parts of the university. Indeed, from the turn of the twenty-first century many junior academics began to give greater weight to their research than their teaching. From the late 1980s the British government, keen to ensure that public money was being well spent, started to audit closely the research activity of the United Kingdom's universities. As government funding for research was pegged to the judgement of the auditors, Oxford dons, like university academics everywhere, were encouraged to maximize their time spent advancing knowledge.

Oxford's postwar commitment to promoting research was particularly evident in the rapid rise in the number of its postgraduate students. From 536 in 1938–9, the number had risen twentyfold to 10,941 in December 2016, a figure little different from the undergraduate total.[83] By that date the two communities looked much the same in terms of gender balance but Oxford's postgraduates were a much more cosmopolitan group. In December 2016, 64 per cent were from overseas. In the 1950s and 1960s there had always been many postgraduates from the Commonwealth and the United States studying at Oxford. In the early twenty-first century postgraduate students came from all over the world. The largest contingent continued to hail from the United States but the second biggest group were normally the Chinese; Germans too were particularly

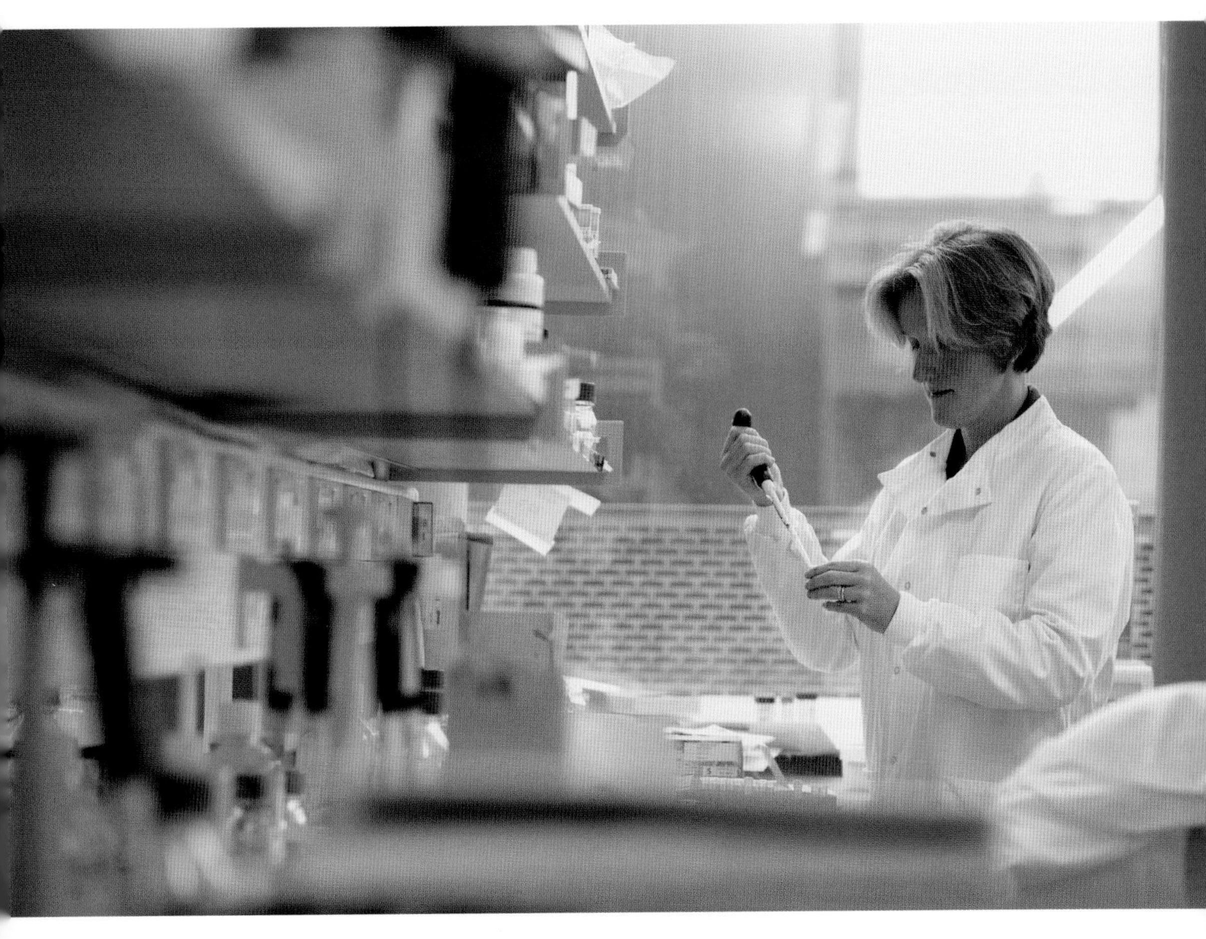

Medical scientist at work in her laboratory, Old Road Campus Research Building, Headington.

visible among European Union nationals.[84] The large number of non-anglophone postgraduates was testimony to Oxford's new-found stature as a research university. This was also evident in the amount of research money it was able to attract from government and private sources. With the novel emphasis from the 1980s on team research, in the arts as well as the sciences, more and more money was made available subject to open competition. In 1987–8 Oxford's income from research grants was £40 million; in 2015–16 it was £537 million, more

First-year undergraduates in a maths and physics lecture.

than any other British university received. On the proceeds, the university was able to employ a growing number of contract research staff, usually postdoctoral researchers, who assisted the dons in their research. There were only 400 in 1975 but 4,972 in July 2016.[85]

In the years following the Second World War Oxford's desire to be seen as a major research university was quickly boosted by the number of Nobel Prizes awarded to its scientists, often for work done or begun before 1939. In the year the war ended Ernst Chain (1906–1979) and Howard Florey (1898–1968) were honoured for their role in the discovery of penicillin. In 1947, 1956 and 1964, Nobels were won by three Oxford chemists, Robert Robinson (1886–1975), Cyril Hinshelwood (1897–1967) and Dorothy Hodgkin (1910–1994). Then in 1972 and 1973 the Prize was awarded to the biochemist Rodney Porter (1917–1985) and to the animal behaviourist Nikolaas Tinbergen (1907–1988). It was given substance, too, by the emergence of a particular Oxford brand of analytic philosophy, pioneered by Gilbert Ryle (1900–1976) and John L. Austin (1911–1960), which studied the meaning and performative power of everyday language. For the first time since the fourteenth century, Oxford was once again a philosophical powerhouse. Oxford anthropology and Oxford history were also at the cutting edge in the 1950s and 1960s. Edward Evans-Pritchard (1902–1973) developed a new understanding of social anthropology based on seeking the internal coherence of tribal belief systems and practices, while Young Turks in the history faculty moved the discipline in Britain away from high politics and towards the study of society and culture.

From the mid 1970s, however, Oxford's lustre appeared to dim. Its economists continued to win Nobel Prizes but the only Oxford scientist awarded the honour after Tinbergen was the geneticist Sir Paul Nurse (b.1949), who won the Prize in 2001, eight years after he had resigned his chair in microbiology and moved to another university. There were no obvious figures in the humanities either who stood out as having revolutionized their field, if a number, such as the Hellenist Martin West (1937–2013), received the prestigious Balzan Prize. But if Oxford in the early twenty-first century no longer harboured any of the world's most creative minds, it continued to produce an enviable number of lesser stars. Indeed, as the number of the universities grew, scientific research was increasingly conducted in international clusters, and many of the top brains were lured to the United States. Oxford was thus unlikely to have shone as brightly in the firmament as it had in the 1950s and 1960s. What cemented its reputation as a top research university in the new millennium was the sheer number of first-rate minds it sheltered. The 2008 government audit made this abundantly clear. In that year, Oxford submitted for appraisal the work of 2,246 permanent academics, contract staff and junior research fellows. Of the forty-eight units of assessment or different disciplinary heads under which a university's research was evaluated, Oxford topped the list in seventeen and was second in six. Thirty-two per cent of Oxford's research activity was judged to be world leading and 70 per cent to be world leading or internationally excellent, a higher proportion than for any of its United Kingdom competitors.[86]

Saïd Business School, 2001–2: funded by the businessman Wafic Rida Saïd (b.1939), it is the first university building seen by visitors to Oxford on leaving the railway station.

CHANGES IN STRUCTURE

Oxford's development into a large world-class research university in the seventy-five years after the Second World War had a dramatic effect on its footprint in the city and surrounding countryside. Until 1939 the university was principally located in the complex of buildings around the Bodleian Library and the Science Area. Besides the university press in Jericho and the women's colleges which had been founded in North Oxford, no part of the university was more than ten minutes' walk from the city centre at Carfax. By 2015 the university had spread its wings. A cluster of new buildings were erected on the Science Area or adjacent sites; in order to house their students, colleges put up residential blocks outside their curtilage; and university faculties and departments took over new areas of the city. In the 1960s the central administration had migrated from the Clarendon Building to larger facilities in Wellington Square. From the late 1970s the fast-expanding medical faculty gradually moved its operations to the new hospitals springing up on Headington Hill, while in 2001 the area around the railway

SAID BUSINESS SCHOOL UNIVERSITY OF OXFORD

station began to be colonized with the establishment of the Saïd Business School. Some science research too moved out into the countryside. From an early date Oxford's physicists found space at Britain's Atomic Energy Research Establishment at Harwell and the Joint European Torus project at Culham, while in the 1990s first Magdalen and then the university set up science parks at Sandford and Begbroke where the practical potential of research in new fields such as biotechnology could be explored and marketed. Most of the university's new buildings erected before 1970 were of limited architectural interest. So too were those put up by the colleges, with the exception of the

Blavatnik School of Government, 2015: a gift of the businessman Leonard Blavatnik (b.1957). Its bold circular design is said to represent democracy and its glass facade political transparency. The Radcliffe Observatory is in the background.

St John's 'Beehive', opened in 1960. With the end of the era of brutalist architecture, however, and a new reliance on donor rather than state funding, Oxford's commissions became more imaginative. Particular gems of the early twenty-first century are the new biochemistry building in the Science Area (2008), the Bodleian's Book Repository at Swindon (2010), and the Blavatnik School of Government in Jericho (2015).

The greatly extended university needed a much larger administrative apparatus to support its activities. Before 1939 the colleges had employed a bevy of clerks, cooks, gardeners and maintenance men, but the university itself had got by with a small secretariat under the control of the registrar, the vice-chancellor's chief official. The university's administration expanded slowly until 1990 but thereafter its numbers exploded. The extensive building programme, the advent of new technology, and the new focus on team research, fundraising, and health and safety at work created an ever-growing demand for new administrators at all levels. The university probably employed 200 non-academic staff in 1939. In July 2016 it employed nearly 6,665. As the colleges had a similar number of staff, some 13,000 individuals were by then looking after the needs of 1,800 academics, 5,000 research staff and 22,000 students.[87] Oxford had begun to resemble a huge business.

Such a large enterprise could no longer be governed in the same way as in the past. Two major weaknesses in the existing system of governance had become apparent by 1960. The first, a criticism levelled at Oxford by Lord Robbins (1898–1984) in his 1963 report to the government on the future of the British university system, was the difficulty it had 'in reaching rapid decisions on matters of policy'.[88] All initiatives by the central administration had to be scrutinized not only by Congregation but also by the individual colleges, which resulted in long delays. The second, identified in the Franks Report three years

Students watching a varsity athletics match at the Sir Roger Bannister athletics track, Oxford, 2016. It was on this track that Bannister ran the first mile under four minutes on 6 May 1954. Photograph by Martin Parr.

later, was the absence of clear lines of responsibility within the university's committee structure. The Hebdomadal Council, nominally in overall charge under Congregation, appeared to have little control over the General Board, which was responsible for teaching, while the General Board seemed unable to lay down the law to the individual faculty boards, which jealously maintained their right to determine the undergraduate curriculum.[89] Subsequent to the Franks Report, Congregation dealt with both problems but only partly. The college input into decision-making was speeded up by the introduction of a Conference of Colleges, where representatives could chew over matters of mutual interest, and Council's powers at the apex of the administrative hierarchy were fully defined. However, as the new intercollegiate committee had no power to bind its constituent members and the faculty boards retained their independence, the changes in governance had limited effect. By the mid 1990s the system, though not in crisis, was in need of further overhaul. The General Board's authority had become particularly problematic: it had no control over the university's research income from grants, which was now larger than its own budget, and one of the faculties, medicine, which employed large numbers of contract staff, had all but escaped from its control. The North Commission advocated root-and-branch reform and Congregation agreed. The General Board was abolished and replaced by a small number of academic boards under Council, called divisions, which oversaw the activities of a cluster of cognate faculties. At the same time, Council was enlarged so that it included for the first time student and college representatives, and its decision-making capacity was improved by the establishment of a number of specialist subcommittees whose duty was to plan in detail every aspect of the university's long-term future. Oxford was to become a proactive rather than a reactive institution.[90]

An attempt to streamline the university's governance even further was taken by Vice-Chancellor John Hood (b.1952) in 2004–06. Hood, Oxford's first vice-chancellor not to be a member of the university on his election, was keen to separate institutional from academic governance by dividing Council into two separate boards, the first a small board of trustees in charge of policy, which would be dominated by outsiders rather than academics.[91] This was needed, he believed, both to improve the efficiency of what was now a huge and complex entity and to bring Oxford in line with other British universities, apart from Cambridge, where ultimate control lay with a small council with a majority of lay members who brought to the table external expertise and an independent point of view. Congregation, however, would have none of it. Oxford from the thirteenth century had been a masters' university, and it was still a masters' university 800 years later. The sovereignty of Congregation was clearly affirmed in both the Franks and the North reports.[92] Though Hood claimed that the dons' authority was not at risk from the new proposals, the large majority of academics were unconvinced. Congregation at the beginning of the twenty-first century continued to meet every two weeks in term time. If much of the business was trivial and the meetings for the most part poorly attended, the dons reserved the right to debate at length and to ultimately reject initiatives from the central administration that they felt harmed Oxford's tradition of self-government. The dons were proud of the continued link with the medieval past and would not surrender their democratic inheritance, as Professor Donald Frazer (b.1949) of Worcester College emphasized in his speech to Congregation on the day Hood's proposals were defeated: 'The issue of governance is quite simple. It was summed up for me by a quietly-spoken colleague. He said there are two issues: (1) it is dangerous to concentrate too much power in the hands of the few; (2) why should we give up something good, merely to conform to some sector norm?'[93]

Beecroft Building: Oxford's first new building for the Department of Physics in fifty years, built to ensure low vibration levels and perfect temperature control. It is located on the Science Area opposite Keble College.

Afterword

Admission of Louise Richardson, Oxford's first female vice-chancellor (b.1959), January 2016: celebratory dinner at Balliol College.

Oxford today is one of the world's leading universities, prized for the high quality of both its undergraduate teaching and its research. Enough has been said in the preceding pages to make it clear that its present greatness did not fall into its lap. In 1850 few observers would have concluded that the Anglican seminary would escape its confessional confines, accept the Humboldtian ideal and blossom a hundred years later into an intellectual powerhouse. Many must have thought that, even after the mid-nineteenth-century reforms, both Oxford and Cambridge were destined at best to become fashionable provincial liberal arts universities. It would be the new University of London that, given its location, would naturally become the chief centre of learning and research in Britain and the empire.[94] That Oxford defied its fate and emerged from the Second World War ready to join the elite of research universities was due to the efforts of a number of singular individuals in the first half of the twentieth century who were committed to making it an intellectual force in the world. Oxford certainly had one thing in its favour. By educating so many members of the establishment, it had influence in the right places: the government of the day, however critical, was usually anxious to assist in its transformation. But, ultimately, it was members of the university and private benefactors who provided the momentum. Curzon, Nuffield and Lindemann were just three of the figures encountered in these pages whose foresight, bounty and opportunism helped lay the foundations of the modern research university.

It took effort and dedication to raise Oxford to its present position and it will be just as hard to keep it there. Oxford can never rest on its laurels. The university world is increasingly competitive and it can only be a matter of time before some of the Chinese universities begin to challenge it for a place in the sun. Moreover, some of the chief factors underlying Oxford's present status are largely outside its control. The university's ability to attract the brightest undergraduates in the longer term is not a given. An Oxford education has always been expensive. For a short period of time between 1960 and 2000, the British government paid students' fees and provided help towards their board and lodging: Oxford benefited from this window to broaden its pattern of recruitment and impose higher entry qualifications. With growing student debt and greater competition for the best jobs on graduation, many potential applicants may no longer feel that an Oxford undergraduate education is worth the investment, especially if cheaper good alternatives exist, as may become the case if new technology is used imaginatively. Oxford's ability to attract ever-increasing research income may also come under threat. Rival universities may prove just as adept at attracting funds, or grant-giving bodies may decide that the future location for research should be the small stand-alone institute rather than the highly bureaucratized multidisciplinary university. It is unlikely, then, that after 800 years Oxford's history has come to an end. At some point in the present century it will have to reinvent itself once more to survive and prosper. The omens, however, are good. Oxford's history has been a story of adaptation. Whatever the future holds, its past suggests it will respond successfully.

Timeline

873 Mythical date of foundation by Alfred the Great

*c.*1095 Opening of the first school of higher learning at Oxford

1214 Recognition of Oxford's schools as a privileged entity and appointment of the first scholars' chancellor

1215–1350 Institutionalization and emergence of a self-governing masters' *studium generale*, or *universitas*, with an elected chancellor, two proctors, and faculties of arts, theology, canon law, civil law and medicine

1274 Foundation of Merton College

1280 First statutes of University College

*c.*1280 Establishment of the first halls

1282 First statutes of Balliol College

1292 Roger Bacon purportedly dies in Oxford

1298–9 Duns Scotus lectures on the *Sentences* of Peter Lombard

1313–19 William of Ockham lectures on the Bible and the *Sentences*

*c.*1314 Foundation of Exeter College

1324 Foundation of Oriel College

1341 Foundation of The Queen's College

1344 Bradwardine completes his *De causa Dei*

1369–72 Wyclif lectures on the Bible and the *Sentences*

1379 Foundation of New College

*c.*1410 All students and masters required to live in a hall or college

1427 Foundation of Lincoln College

1438 Foundation of All Souls College

1458 Foundation of Magdalen College

1488 Completion of the Divinity School

*c.*1500 Division of the masters' *congregatio magna* and *minor* into Convocation and Congregation

1509 Foundation of Brasenose College

1517 Foundation of Corpus Christi College

1535 Closure of the regular colleges and the teaching of canon law forbidden

1540 Endowment of chairs in Greek, Hebrew, civil law and theology by Henry VIII

1546 Foundation of Christ Church

1555 Foundation of Trinity College and St John's College

1556 Execution of Archbishop Cranmer outside Balliol

1569 Vice-chancellor, heads of house and senior masters given the right to vet the business of Convocation and Congregation

1571 Foundation of Jesus College

1581 Loyalty oath to the Church of England demanded of all students on arrival

1602 Bodleian Library opens

1604 University given the right to elect two MPs

1610 Foundation of Wadham College

1614 Completion of the Schools Quadrangle

1621 Foundation of the Botanic Garden

1624 Foundation of Pembroke College

1631 Establishment of the Hebdomadal Board chaired by the vice-chancellor and staffed by the college heads: further erosion of the power of Convocation and Congregation

1636 The Laudian Code sums up the university's existing statutes

1650s Oxford becomes a centre of the new science

1660–1800 Virtual disappearance of the faculties of theology, civil law and medicine

1669 Sheldonian Theatre opens

1683 Old Ashmolean Museum opens

1687 Expulsion for disobedience of the fellows of Magdalen by James II

1713 Clarendon Building opens

1714 Foundation of Worcester College

1744 John Wesley accuses the whole university of corruption in a sermon at St Mary's Church

1749 Radcliffe Camera opens

1772 Founding stone of Radcliffe Observatory laid

1800 Examination statute implemented: new regulations governing BA and MA degrees and the introduction of classified degrees

1829 Rejection of Sir Robert Peel as the university's MP after his support for Catholic Emancipation; first Oxford and Cambridge boat race

1841 John Henry Newman's Tract 90 declaring the faith of the Church of England to be compatible with Roman Catholicism

1850 BA exam divided into four separate tracks, including mathematics and natural science; to gain the degree, students have to pass in Literae Humaniores (classics and philosophy) and one other discipline

1850 Royal Commission set up to drag the university into the nineteenth century

1854 Parliamentary reform statute enacted, whereby Congregation becomes the university's dominant legislative body and the Hebdomadal Board/ Council its chief executive; the power of the college heads on Council is clipped; college fellowships opened to competition; students of any religion allowed to attend

1860 University Museum opens for teaching in science

1868–9 Students allowed to study at Oxford without belonging to a college or hall (until the 1960s)

1870 Foundation of Keble College

1871 Fellows no longer have to be celibate

1874 Royal Commission set up to look at the university's and colleges' wealth; foundation of Hertford College (formerly Magdalen Hall)

1877 Royal Commission set up to overhaul the university's and colleges' statutes

1879 First women's colleges open: Lady Margaret Hall and Somerville

1881 College wealth taxed to allow the creation of more university posts

1882 Establishment of a new faculty structure with the creation of four faculty boards: arts, natural science (including medicine), law and theology; by 1966 the number of faculties had grown to sixteen (divided in turn into sub-faculties and departments)

1882 New university statutes: university post-holders expected to pursue research

1884 Foundation of the Pitt Rivers Museum

1886 End of the compulsory study of classics for undergraduates; St Hugh's College opens (for women)

1893 St Hilda's College opens (for women)

1896 Campion Hall opens (for Jesuits), the first Roman Catholic community to be established at Oxford since the Reformation

1902 Rhodes Scholarships established

1908 Foundation of the Ashmolean Museum of Art and Archaeology

1912 Establishment of the General Board under Council to oversee the faculties

1917 Introduction of the DPhil degree

1919 Royal Commission set up to look at Oxford's social intake and research profile

1920 Female undergraduates allowed to take a degree

1921 The chemist Frederick Soddy wins Oxford's first Nobel Prize

1922 University receives a state subsidy for the first time

1924 Museum of the History of Science opens in the Old Ashmolean building

1928 Foundation of St Peter's College

1936 Establishment of the Institute of Medical Research and School of Clinical Medicine

1937 Foundation of Nuffield College, the first postgraduate college, and the first for both men and women, specializing in the social sciences

1945 New Bodleian opens

1950 Foundation of St Antony's College (for postgraduates)

1952 Foundation of St Anne's College (for women) and St Edmund Hall (for men; the last medieval hall)

1962 Foundation of St Catherine's College (for men) and Linacre College (for postgraduates)

1963 Nobel Prize won by animal behaviourist Nikolaas Tinburgen (the last Oxford scientist to win a Nobel while in post)

1964–66 Franks Commission: internal inquiry into the modernization of Oxford

1965 Foundation of Wolfson College and St Cross College, both for postgraduates

1974 Five men's colleges admit women

1979 Foundation of Green College (for postgraduates) for medicine; most men's and women's colleges go co-educational

1983 Foundation of Templeton College (for postgraduates) for business and management

1994 Foundation of Kellogg College

1994–97 North Commission: internal inquiry into streamlining Oxford's governance, which confirms the sovereignty of Congregation

1995 Foundation of Mansfield College, initially established in 1886 as a hall for Congregationalists

1996 Foundation of Harris Manchester College (for mature students), a hall from 1989

2000 Abolition of the General Board and the grouping of the faculties into four academic divisions answerable to a restructured Council under Congregation

2001 Saïd Business School opens

2008 St Hilda's, the only surviving single-sex college, accepts men; Green and Templeton Colleges merge

2010–11 Oxford ranked second in the *Times Higher Education* World University Rankings

2015 Blavatnik School of Government opens

NOTES

FOREWORD

1 An annual ceremony dating from the early eighteenth century where the university remembers the blessings bestowed on it by its many benefactors and honorary degrees are awarded to prominent figures in politics and the arts and sciences.

THE MEDIEVAL UNIVERSITY

2 The document is transcribed in H.E. Salter, *Medieval Archives of Oxford*, 2 vols, Oxford, 1920, vol. I, pp. 2–4.

3 Estimates for the numbers at the medieval university vary. The most recent are found in T.H. Aston, 'Oxford's Medieval Alumni', *Past and Present*, vol. 74, 1977, pp. 6–8.

4 These are printed in *Statuta antiqua universitatis Oxoniensis*, ed. Strickland Gibson, Oxford, 1931.

5 The *Sentences* was a twelfth-century textbook which explained and resolved a series of doctrinal problems, the *Decretum* a collection of church pronouncements clarified and reconciled by a twelfth-century Bolognese jurist, the *Decretals* a collection of papal bulls and rescripts, the sixth-century *Code* the emperor Justinian's codification of the decisions of his imperial predecessors, and the *Digest* a collection of judgments by Roman jurisconsults. No specific texts were set for medicine but it can be assumed that the course was built around the extant works of Galen and Hippocrates and the *Canon* of the Muslim philosopher Avicenna (980–1037).

6 A deacon was a clerk in minor orders.

7 Heads of Oxford colleges had and have various titles: warden, master, provost, president, rector and principal.

8 *Statuta*, ed. Gibson, p. 208.

9 *Statuta*, ed. Gibson, pp. 574–88; on games, p. 576.

10 Scholars in Magdalen were called demies because they received half board; in Corpus they were called disciples.

11 *Statutes of Magdalen College, Oxford*, in *Statutes of the Colleges of Oxford*, 3 vols, London, 1853, vol. 2, pp. 60 and 73.

12 *Register of the University of Oxford*, ed. C.W. Boase, vol. 1, Oxford, 1885, pp. xxii–xxv.

13 *Statutes of Cardinal College*, in *Statutes*, vol. 2, pp. 127–8.

14 *Statuta*, ed. Gibson, pp. 221–2.

THE ANGLICAN SEMINARY

15 'Introductions', *Register of the University of Oxford*, vol. 2, part 1, ed. Andrew Clark, Oxford, 1887, pp. 167–8.

16 After the Interregnum, radical Protestants who wanted an end to bishops as well as liturgical reform formed their own underground churches. Under the 1689 Act of Toleration most dissenters gained the right to worship openly.

17 Words of the All Souls lawyer Sir William Blackstone (1723–1780), cited in V.H.H. Green, *The Commonwealth of Lincoln College 1427–1977*, Oxford, 1979, p. 349.

18 *Remarks on Certain Passages in the Thirty-Nine Articles*, Tracts for the Times, no. 90, London, 1841, esp. chs 2 and 3.

19 The university had already agreed on 27 June 1534, after royal prompting, that the bishop of Rome had no authority in England.

20 Angus Macintyre, 'The College, King James II and the Revolution 1687–1688', in Laurence Brockliss, Gerald Harriss and Angus Macintyre, *Magdalen College and the Crown: Essays for the Tercentenary of the Restoration of the College 1688*, Magdalen College, Oxford, 1988, ch. 2, at p. 56.

21 *Statuta*, ed. Gibson, pp. 570, 561–5.

22 His opponent won by 755 to 609 votes. For the votes cast, see *An Authentic Copy of a Poll to Serve in Parliament for the University of Oxford*, Oxford, 1829.

23 *Register of the University of Oxford*, ed. C.W. Boase, vol. 1, Oxford, 1885, pp. xxi–xxv.

24 Lawrence Stone, 'The Size and Composition of the Oxford Student Body 1580–1910', in Stone (ed.), *The University in Society*, vol. 1: *Oxford and Cambridge from the 14th to the Early 19th Century*, Princeton, NJ, 1975, pp. 6 and 91 (graph and table).

25 J. Heywood, 'Statistics of the Universities of Oxford and Cambridge', *Quarterly Journal of the Statistical Society of London*, vol. v, 1842, p. 243.

26 Robin Darwall-Smith, 'The Monks of Magdalen, 1688–1854', in L.W.B. Brockliss (ed.), *Magdalen College Oxford: A History*, Oxford, 2008, p. 285.

27 *Statutes of the University of Oxford Codified in the Year 1636 under the Authority of Archbishop Laud, Chancellor of the University*, ed. J. Griffiths, Oxford, 1888, pp. 33–42, 45–6.

28 *Oxford University Statutes*, trans. G.R. Ward and James Heywood, 2 vols, London, 1845, vol. II, pp. 31–7, 61–5.

29 Christ Church was a peculiar college. It had no foundation statutes; it was governed by the cathedral chapter, not its fellows; and the fellows, confusingly, were called students.

30 That is, students not on the foundation who paid for their board and lodging. They were called commoners, whatever their social status, because they took their meals in common in the college hall.

31 *Statutes* (1853), vol. 2: *Statutes of Magdalen*, pp. 60, 73.

32 Before 1600 fellows received little from their college beyond free board and lodging. As the return from the endowment increased over the next 250 years, the 'profits' were shared out between them. In the early nineteenth century most fellows could expect a dividend of at least £100 (L.W.B. Brockliss, *The University of Oxford: A History*, Oxford, 2016, pp. 282–3).

33 Obadiah Walker, *Of Education, especially of Young Gentlemen*, Oxford, 1673, p. 122.

34 *The Autobiographies of Edward Gibbon*, ed. John Murray, London, 1896, pp. 77, 81.

35 *The Letters and Diaries of John Henry Newman*, ed. I.T. Ker, vol. 1, Oxford, 1978, pp. 43, 49, 92.

36 G.L'E. Turner, 'Experimental Sciences in Early Nineteenth-Century Oxford', *History of Universities*, vol. 8, 1989, pp. 117–35.

37 Isaac Newton (1642–1727) developed his universal law of attraction while at Cambridge in the 1670s and 1680s.

38 William Harvey (1578–1657) was a Cambridge-trained royal doctor who made his discovery in London; he was briefly warden of Merton in the mid 1640s.

39 The editor, Charles Boyle (1676–1731), thought the text, a series of letters, dated from the sixth century BCE, when in the fact they were from the second century CE.

40 Maimonides' fourteen-volume *Mishneh Torah* was the most important medieval codification of Talmudic law.

41 The *Edinburgh Review* was the voice of moderate reform in the first half of the nineteenth century: it wanted an end to the Anglican monopoly in public life and an extension of the parliamentary franchise.

42 William Hamilton, 'On the State of the English Universities with More Especial Reference to Oxford', in *Discussions on Philosophy and Literature, Education and University Reform Chiefly from the 'Edinburgh Review'*, 2nd edn, London, 1853, pp. 416–17.

43 *Angliae notitia*, 20th edn, London, 1702, p. 449.

44 Publishers were unwilling to take on academic books lest they failed to find a market. Oxford University Press made a handsome return from printing Bibles and other religious works, and used the profits to subsidize scholarly tomes.

45 Zacharias Conrad von Uffenbach, *Oxford in 1710*, trans. W.H. Quarrell and J.C. Quarrell, Oxford, 1928, p. 9.

OXFORD IN THE AGE OF EMPIRE

46 The other nine were London, Durham, Birmingham, Bristol, Leeds, Liverpool, Manchester, Reading and Sheffield. London from 1898 was a federal university with affiliates in the capital and the provinces, such as Imperial College and the London School of Economics.

47 They were called 'schools' after the rooms in the Schools Quadrangle where candidates were examined.

48 Until 1920 they had to show an acquaintance with Greek too.

49 On the eve of the First World War 30 per cent of Oxford students still took no degree at all.

50 *Royal Commission appointed to enquire into the property and income of the University and Colleges of Oxford*, Parliamentary Papers 1852 (1482), xxii, *Report*, p. 33.

51 Wycliffe Hall, evangelicals (1877); Mansfield, Congregationalists (1886); Manchester, Unitarians (1893); Campion Hall, Jesuits (1896); St Benet's, Benedictines (1899); Greyfriars, Franciscans (1910); Blackfriars, Dominicans (1921); Regent's Park, Baptists (1926).

52 G.N. Curzon, *Principles and Methods of University Reform*, Oxford, 1909, pp. 53, 70.

53 The scholarships too no longer fully covered an undergraduate's costs of board and lodging as they had done when they were first established in the Late Middle Ages.

54 A.T. Denning, *The Family Story*, London, 1981, p. 34.

55 R.D. Anderson, 'Universities and Elites in Modern Britain', *History of Universities*, vol. 10, 1991, pp. 234–5 (tables).

56 Edward Copleston, *A Reply to the Calumnies of the Edinburgh Review against Oxford containing an Account of the Studies Pursued in the University*, 2nd edn, Oxford, 1810, esp. ch. 3.

57 John Henry Newman, *The Idea of a University*, ed. Frank M. Turner, New Haven, CT, 1996 (first edn 1873).

58 Geoffrey Faber, *Jowett*, London, 1957, p. 167.

59 G.H. Martin and J.R.L. Highfield, *A History of Merton College, Oxford*, Oxford, 1997, pp. 328–9.

60 *The History of the University of Oxford*, vol. VII: *Nineteenth-Century Oxford*, part 2, ed. M.G. Brock and M.C. Curthoys, Oxford, 2000, p. 283.

61 Malcolm Tozier, *The Ideal of Manliness: The Legacy of Thring's Uppingham*, Truro, 2015, ch. 1.

62 Herbert Warren, *College Unity*, Oxford, 1885, p. 3.

63 John Buxton and Penry Williams (eds), *New College Oxford 1379–1979*, Oxford, 1979, p. 135.

64 M. Pattison, *Suggestions on Academical Organisation with Especial Reference to Oxford*, Edinburgh, 1868, pp. 171–2.

65 Curzon, *Principles and Methods*, p. 180.

66 Oxford, Magdalen College Archives, FD/11, sub L.E. Sutton, MS letter L.E. Sutton to President Gordon, 5 May 1934.

67 The New Bodleian, designed by Sir Giles Gilbert Scott (1880–1960), officially opened in 1945.

THE WORLD UNIVERSITY

68 www.hesa.ac.uk/data-and-analysis/students/whos-in-he; www.hesa.ac.uk/news/19-01-2017/sfr243-staff; www.hesa.ac.uk/news/02-03-2017/income-and-expenditure, accessed 22 February 2018.

69 Brockliss, *Oxford*, p. 767 (table); www.ox.ac.uk/about/organisation/finance-and-funding?wssl=1, accessed 10 August 2017.

70 From the Latin *dominus*: lord or master.

71 None of the other denominational halls of the late nineteenth century made the transition, which required both an endowment and a readiness to admit students of all religious backgrounds or none.

72 Green and Templeton were merged in 2008.

73 Initially Manchester College and Rewley House. They were put on a firm footing thanks to the carpet retailer Lord Harris of Peckham and the Kellogg Foundation. Oxford had been offering outreach courses from the late nineteenth century.

74 Oxford and Cambridge were the only two European universities ranked in the top ten; the others were all American – Harvard, Stanford, Berkeley, MIT, Caltech, Columbia, Princeton and Chicago.

75 www.ox.ac.uk/about/facts-and-figures/student-numbers?wssl=1, accessed 10 August 2017.

76 In December 2016 it was 46.8 per cent.

77 University of Oxford, *Report of Commission of Enquiry* [Franks Report], 2 vols, Oxford, 1966, vol. I, p. 78; 'Financial Support for Undergraduates', circulated university document, author's archive, 2012. With the development of the services economy post-1980, the working class ceased to be a significant section of the population. A better measure of Oxford's social profile thereafter was income.

78 *Corporate Plan 2005–6 to 2009–10*, Oxford, 2005, pp. 10, 11 (draft for Congregation, author's archive).

79 www.ox.ac.uk/about/facts-and-figures/student-numbers?wssl=1, as at December 2016, accessed 7 April 2017.

80 *Report of Commission of Enquiry* [Franks Report], vol. I, pp. 102–16.

81 University of Oxford, *Commission of Inquiry Report* [North Report], Oxford, 1997, p. 132.

82 Brockliss, *Oxford*, p. 766 (table); www.admin.ox.ac.uk/media/global/wwwadminoxacuk/localsites/personnel/documents/factsandfigures/staffingfigures2016/Table_1.pdf, accessed 10 August 2017.

83 Brockliss, *Oxford*, p. 763 (table); www.ox.ac.uk/about/facts-and-figures/student-numbers?wssl=1, accessed 10 August 2017.

84 Brockliss, *Oxford*, p. 763 (table). In December 2016 the German contingent slightly outnumbered the Chinese: www.ox.ac.uk/about/facts-and-figures/student-numbers?wssl=1, accessed 10 August 2017.

85 Brockliss, *Oxford*, pp. 766–7 (tables); www.ox.ac.uk/about/organisation/finance-and-funding?wssl=1, accessed 10 August 2017; www.admin.ox.ac.uk/media/global/wwwadminoxacuk/localsites/personnel/documents/factsandfigures/staffingfigures2016/Table_1.pdf, accessed 10 August 2017.

86 www.ox.ac.uk/research/rae_2008_results, accessed 8 April 2013.

87 Brockliss, *Oxford*, p. 766 (table); www.admin.ox.ac.uk/media/global/wwwadminoxacuk/localsites/personnel/documents/factsandfigures/staffingfigures2016/Table_1.pdf, accessed 10 August 2017.

88 Committee on Higher Education, *Report of the Committee Appointed by the Prime Minister under the Chairmanship of Lord Robbins 1961–63* [Robbins Report], London, 1963, p. 224.

89 *Report of Commission of Enquiry* [Franks Report], vol. I, ch. 6.

90 *Commission of Inquiry Report* [North Report], ch. 5.

91 *White Paper on University Governance*, Oxford, 2006.

92 *Report of Commission of Enquiry* [Franks Report], vol. I, pp. 230–36; *Commission of Inquiry Report* [North Report], p. 67.

93 *Oxford University Gazette*, supplement 1, 22 November 2006, p. 409.

AFTERWORD

94 For example, Richard B. Haldane, *Education and the Empire*, London, 1902, pp. 34–6. Haldane (1856–1928) was a Liberal and later a Labour politician.

FURTHER READING

UNIVERSITY OF OXFORD

Brockliss, L.W.B, *The University of Oxford: A History*, Oxford, 2017.

The History of the University of Oxford, 8 vols, Oxford, 1984–2000.

Volume I: *The Early Oxford Schools*, ed. J.I. Catto, Oxford, 1984.

Volume II: *Late Medieval Oxford*, ed. J.I. Catto and T.A.R. Evans, Oxford, 1992.

Volume III: *The Collegiate University*, ed. James McConica, Oxford, 1986.

Volume IV: *Seventeenth-Century Oxford*, ed. Nicholas Tyacke, Oxford, 1997.

Volume V: *The Eighteenth Century*, ed. L.S. Sutherland and L.G. Mitchell, Oxford, 1986.

Volume VI: *Nineteenth-Century Oxford*, part 1, ed. M.G. Brock and M.C. Curthoys, Oxford, 1997.

Volume VII: *Nineteenth-Century Oxford*, part 2, ed. M.G. Brock and M.C. Curthoys, Oxford, 2000.

Volume VIII: *The Twentieth Century*, ed. Brian Harrison, Oxford, 1994.

THE COLLEGES

Adams, Pauline, *Somerville for Women: An Oxford College 1879–1993*, Oxford, 1996.

Brockliss, L.W.B. (ed.), *Magdalen College Oxford: A History*, Oxford, 2008.

Buxton, John, and Penry Williams (eds), *New College Oxford 1379–1979*, Oxford, 1979.

Catto, Jeremy (ed.), *Oriel College: A History*, Oxford, 2013.

Crook, J. Mordaunt, *Brasenose: The Biography of an Oxford College*, Oxford, 2008.

Curthoys, Judith, *The Cardinal's College: Christ Church, Chapter and Verse*, London, 2012.

Darwall-Smith, Robin, *A History of University College Oxford*, Oxford, 2008.

Davies, C.S.L., and Jane Garnett, *Wadham College*, Oxford, 1994.

Green, Vivian H.H., *The Commonwealth of Lincoln College 1427–1977*, Oxford, 1979.

Hopkins, Clare, *Trinity: 450 years of an Oxford College Community*, Oxford, 2005.

Jones, John, *Balliol College: A History*, 2nd edn, Oxford, 1997.

Kaye, Elaine, *Mansfield College Oxford: Its Origin, History and Significance*, Oxford, 1996.

Kelly, J.N.D., *St Edmund Hall: Almost Seven Hundred Years*, Oxford, 1989.

Martin, G.H., and J.R.L. Highfield, *A History of Merton College, Oxford*, Oxford, 1997.

Schwartz, Laura, *A Serious Endeavour: Gender, Education and Community at St Hugh's, 1886–2011*, London, 2011.

PICTURE CREDITS

FRONTISPIECE

© Greg Smolonski

FOREWORD

6 © Ashmolean Museum, University of Oxford, WA2016.48
9 © Cliff Hide

THE MEDIEVAL UNIVERSITY

13 Oxford, Bodleian Library / Oxford University Archives, WPβ/P/12/1
14 © British Library Board / Bridgeman Images
17 The Warden and Fellows of Merton College Oxford
18–19 Oxford, Bodleian Library, Arch.Antiq. A II.13
20 Oxford, Bodleian Library, MS. Bodl. 211, fol. 5r
22 Oxford, Bodleian Library, MS. Bodl. 13 (part 1), fol. 12v
25 Oxford, Bodleian Library, MS. Top. Oxon c. 16, fol. 134r
27 Oxford, Bodleian Library, MS. Fairfax 11, fol. 100r
28 Courtesy of the Warden and Scholars of New College, Oxford / Bridgeman Images
30 Oxford, Bodleian Library, Johnson c.24, vol. 1
33 Oxford, Bodleian Library, Sackler Library Rare Book Room XXXVI.C.[fol.]
34–5 © David Iliff

THE ANGLICAN SEMINARY

40–41 Oxford, Bodleian Library, Sackler Library Rare Book Room XXXVI.C.[fol.]
43 Wikimedia Commons
44–5 Oxford, Bodleian Library, Arch.Antiq. A II.13
47 Oxford, Bodleian Library, LP 78
48–9 The Warden and Fellows of Merton College Oxford
50 Oxford, Bodleian Library / Oxford University Archives, Long Box 21/2
52 Oxford, Bodleian Library, Gough Oxon 109 (1)
55 Oxford, Bodleian Library / Oxford University Archives, WPγ/25c/I, fol. 92
57 Oxford, Bodleian Library, LP 104
58 Oxford, Bodleian Library / Oxford University Archives, SP 37, pp. 468–9
62 Oxford, Bodleian Library, Lister E 7, schem. 9, facing p. 93
65 Oxford, Bodleian Library, MS. Top. Oxon c. 16, fol. 137v
66–7 © Shutterstock / FenlioQ
71 © National Portrait Gallery, London
72 Oxford, Bodleian Library, G.A. Oxon a.92

OXFORD IN THE AGE OF EMPIRE

77 Courtesy of The Lewis Walpole Library, Yale University
78 Yale Center for British Art, Paul Mellon Collection
81 © National Portrait Gallery, London
82 Oxford, Bodleian Library, G.A. Oxon 4° 369
85 The Master and Fellows, Balliol College
86–7 © Oxford University Museum of Natural History
88–9 Wikimedia Commons / Steve Cadman
90–91 By kind permission of the Principal and Fellows of Lady Margaret Hall, Oxford
93 © National Portrait Gallery, London
94 © Oxford University Images / Oxfordshire History Centre
97 © Oxford University Images / Oxfordshire History Centre
99 © Oxford University Images / Oxfordshire History Centre
103 Wikimedia Commons / SBA73

THE WORLD UNIVERSITY

108–9 Oxford, Bodleian Library
111 John Cairns / St Catherine's College, Oxford
114 © Oxford University Images / Greg Smolonski
116 Oxford, Bodleian Library
119 © Oxford University Images / John Cairns Photography
120 © Oxford University Images / Rob Judges Photography
123 © Oxford University Images / David Fisher
124 © Oxford University Images / Stuart Bebb
126 © Martin Parr / Magnum Photos
129 Architect Hawkins / Brown, CGI image Visualisation One
130 © Oxford University Images / John Cairns Photography

INDEX